THE CYCLIST'S MANUAL

THE CYCLIST'S MANUAL

**DOUG COLLIGAN
& DICK TERESI**

STERLING PUBLISHING CO., INC.   NEW YORK

The Cyclist's Manual
was produced and prepared by

Quarto Marketing, Ltd.
212 Fifth Avenue,
New York, N.Y. 10010

Printed and bound in the United States of America by the Maple-Vail Group
Jacket printed by Longacre Press
Typesetting by BPE Graphics

Editors: Wendy Ruoff and John Smallwood
Design: Ken Diamond
Illustrations: Randall Lieu

Published in the United States and Canada by
Sterling Publishing Co., Inc.
Two Park Avenue, New York, N.Y. 10016

Library of Congress Cataloging in Publication Data:
Colligan and Teresi
The Cyclist's Manual
Includes index

CONTENTS

Chapter 1

CHOOSING A BICYCLE

"What bike should I buy?" is a question we hear all the time. And we know the kind of answer that's expected. People want the names of specific brands and models, such as Peugeot U08, Frejus Supercorsa, Schwinn LeTour, Fuji Finest. They want a simple, direct answer but don't expect any simple, direct answers from us. We don't recommend specific brands and models to our friends and neighbors, and we're not going to do it here either. For a simple reason—we can't. Why not? Quality is subject to swift and unpredictable changes. For instance, back in the early 1970s, a well-known French bicycle gained widespread distribution in the United States. It was, in fact, a good, reasonably priced bicycle. Then the bike boom hit, and demand for the bike mushroomed. The manufacturer obviously had to produce the bicycle at too fast a rate and then compounded the problem by starting to use cheaper, seamed tubing on the frame.

Yet, the bike continued to sell well, thanks to word-of-mouth recommendations from cyclists who had the good models from the late 1960s and early 1970s. Similar scenarios were acted out at other companies as well.

Another reason it's difficult to cite specific brands and models is that the parts on them are not always standardized. Brand-name manufacturers, such as Motobecane, Fuji, Carlton, or Schwinn, really only make one item on the bicycle from scratch—the frame. (And even then they buy the tubes ready-made from another supplier.) Everything else on the bike comes from parts manufacturers: the wheel hubs, spokes and rims, the gear shifters, the handlebars, saddle, brakes, and so on. What you're paying the manufacturers for is their ability in soldering or welding the frame together, their judgment in selecting good compatible components, and their care in assembling all these elements into a finished bicycle.

But manufacturers often change the selection of parts from one bike to the next. For example, let's say a manufacturer normally uses a metal Sun Tour derailleur on an El Speedo 10-speed bike. But demand for Sun Tour derailleurs is high and sufficient supplies can't be obtained. So the manufacturer switches to plastic Simplex derailleurs. Which explains why your El Speedo has a totally different kind of derailleur than your neighbor's El Speedo. You haven't been cheated because there's no such thing as a Motobecane brake or a Fuji derailleur. On the other hand, this does change the nature of the bicycle. And it means you must be able to judge bicycles and their individual parts.

There are some brands that can be recommended over others. Schwinns are consistently good, though expensive and a bit heavy. Motobecane has made a good mid-priced bicycle consistently over the years. And it's hard to fault the high-priced racing bicycles of Frejus, Falcon, Colnago, and many others. In fact, there are several more brands in all price categories. But there's yet another reason for not citing specific brands—you can't always get them. There are hundreds of acceptable brands, but it's doubtful that any one bike store is going to carry more than five or six of them. So, if you decide beforehand that you will settle for nothing but a Raleigh, you may find yourself traveling many miles to get it.

Ultimately, what you must do is turn yourself into a quick expert on frames, components, workmanship, and service, and forget about specific manufacturers for the moment. This chapter will help you become that quick expert.

The basic 10-speed bicycle has increasingly become the most popular bike for everyone, from beginners to serious touring cyclists. Its range of gears, lightness and general performance give it a versatility that riders find appealing.

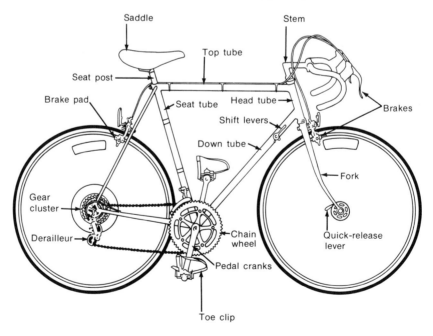

10-SPEED BICYCLES

For most serious cyclists who plan to cycle-tour or camp, or anyone planning day trips of 50 miles (80 kilometers) or longer, the 10-speed is the way to go. One-speeds and 3-speeds are actually better bikes in many circumstances, and we'll discuss them at the end of the chapter.

Where to Buy

The first decision you must make as a prospective 10-speed owner is where to buy the bike. The not-so-obvious answer is a bike store. Not so obvious because there are other alternatives: prime among them are mail-order services, discount stores, and other department stores. Rule out mail order if you are not skilled in assembling the bike yourself. Rule out discount houses because, even though the bicycles there are fully assembled, unless you can be sure that they have been assembled with true professionalism. Of course, the bulk of assembly is done at the factory. But often a bicycle is then shipped to a store with one or even both wheels unattached, the handlebars separate from the frame, brake and derailleur cables unfastened, and so on. Few discount houses will have a full-time bike mechanic putting their bikes together for them but rather a general sort of employee who knows very little about bikes. And it's a rare discount house that will service the bike for you later.

Stick to bike stores. Many of them are not so good either, but at least the odds are improved that you'll find a good mechanic and knowledgeable dealer there.

Size

A bike's size is determined by the length of the seat tube and is usually stated in inches (most bikes measure from 19 to 25 inches) or centimeters (48 to 64 centimeters is normal). Don't confuse this with wheel size, which on adult bikes is usually either 26 or 27 inches (700 millimeters, called 700C)

In any case, the best way to measure a bike is to ignore the numbers and straddle the top tube with both your feet flat on the ground (don't sit on the saddle). You should have a ½- to 1-inch (1- to 2½-centimeter) clearance between your crotch and the tube. If you can't find a bike exactly in this range, compromise by getting one too small rather than too large for obvious safety reasons. We recommend so-called men's bikes for everyone—men, women, girls, and boys—because they're stronger. But if you really want a woman's bike (the kind with no top tube), fit yourself to a man's bike, find out what size it is, then find a woman's bike of the same size.

Frame

There are countless numbers of bikes with different combinations of frames and parts currently on the market. Many things divide the bad from the acceptable, the acceptable from the good, and the good from the very good. But quality begins with the frame.

When Leonardo da Vinci's notebooks were discovered a few years ago, scholars were amazed to find drawings of bicycles with frames very similar to those used today. And indeed, the basic structure of the bike frame has changed little over the years. Perhaps this explains why no one looks closely at the structure when deciding which bike to buy.

Yet, it is the frame that will decide how your bicycle rides, steers, and feels; whether it will be responsive to each thrust of the pedals or absorb all your energy; whether it will track straight, even with hands off the handlebars; and whether it will be heavy and burdensome or lightweight yet strong.

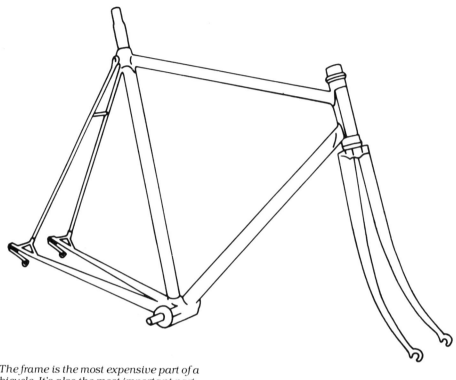

The frame is the most expensive part of a bicycle. It's also the most important part because it mainly determines the durability and ride given by the bike.

There are two basic things to look at in a frame: the kinds of tubes used, and how they're constructed.

There are nine tubes and two blades in a frame. The basic structural tubes are the top, seat, down, and head tubes. These make up the main diamond of the bike. Behind this are the two seat stays and two chain stays that make up the rear triangle. At bottom is a large, short, horizontal tube called the bottom bracket. This tube holds the spindle, the axle on which the pedal cranks revolve. Up front are the two fork blades—not technically considered part of the frame, but most manufacturers make their own forks and use the same kinds of metal and brand of tubing as used for the rest of the frame.

The vast majority of bicycle tubes are made of steel. But the kind of steel used is important, as is the technique used to form it into a round tube. The very cheapest tubes are made of low-carbon rather than high-carbon steel and are seamed. As manufacturers don't advertise that their frames are made of low-carbon steel, or label it as such, ask the bike shop dealer about this. You can, however, tell whether or not the tubes are seamed. *Seamed tubing* is formed simply by wrapping a sheet of steel lengthwise and welding it where the two edges meet. You should be able to see, or at least feel, the seam in a tube. Look at the bottoms or backs of the main tubes as the maker will try to conceal the seam. Look at the chain and seat stays also;

some makers put seamless tubes on the main part of the frame and then skimp on the rear. A frame made with low-carbon steel and seamed tubing is of inferior quality.

Better bicycles will have seamless tubes of high-carbon steel. In the moderate price range, the tubes will be *straight gauge*, that is, the same thickness their entire length. As you go up in price, you will find *double-butted tubes*, which are thicker at both ends than in the middle. Since most of the stress is borne by the joints of the frames, where the ends of the tubes meet, butting makes a lot of sense. Double-butted tubes should be clearly labeled as this is a big selling point. You won't be able to see or feel the butting, because it's done on the inside of the tubes, not the outside, which remains uniform in thickness the entire length.

Also, as the price increases you find finer and finer steels being used. The best bicycles are made with chrome-molybdenum steel (chrome moly) tubing or manganese-molybdenum steel tubing. This is the material that racers insist on and which well-heeled touring cyclists have come to love. Some brands of super tubes are Reynolds of England, Vitus of France, Columbus of Italy, and Ishiwata of Japan.

More exotic materials are also used: titanium, aluminum, graphite, carbon-boron, and other composites. Once you start looking at frames made of these materials, you can expect a price for the complete bicycle of $1,000 or £500 and upwards. (More about these later in the chapter, where we cover custom bikes.)

What makes expensive steel or titanium tubes better than seamed tubing? Basically, what you're paying for is lightness and strength. A very light manganese-molybdenum steel frame, for example, though it weighs considerably less than a low-carbon steel frame, will be much stronger—strong enough for muscular cyclists to ride the bike up the sides of mountains without the bike breaking or failing.

The differences in weights may not seem that staggering to you. A cheap frame may weigh only 7 pounds (3 kilograms), while the best double-butted frames hit somewhere around 4½ pounds (2 kilograms). The aluminum, titanium, and graphite frames all weigh under 3½ pounds (1½ kilograms). But because of costs in general, these small differences are magnified in the construction of the bicycle. What happens is that the manufacturer tends to put cheap heavy parts on a cheap heavy frame. So that heavy frame ends up being a 35-, 40-, or even 50-pound (16-, 18-, or 22-kilogram) bicycle. And expensive light parts go on an expensive light frame,

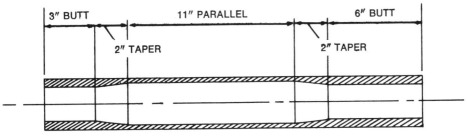

3″ BUTT **11″ PARALLEL** **6″ BUTT**

2″ TAPER **2″ TAPER**

A butted tube doesn't look any different from the outside, but it can withstand much higher pressures than other types of tubes. Invented in 1897 by a nailmaker named Alfred Reynolds, the butting process is also used for manufacturing aircraft parts.

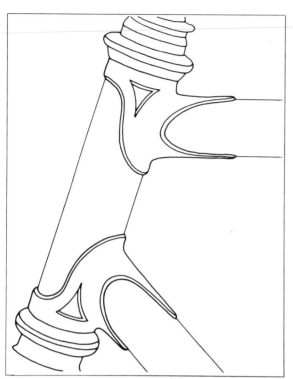

Lugs may not be a guarantee of the quality of a bike's frame, but they can sometimes provide clues if you know what to look for. Examine the edges of a lug on a silver-soldered bike—the tube-lug joint should be perfectly smooth without tell-tale globs of solder.

which ends up being an 18- to 23-pound (8- to 10-kilogram) bicycle. And the in-between frames, as you might expect, fall in the middle.

A word of caution: Despite the fact that quality normally increases with price, seekers of excellence should know that the very expensive frames are not necessarily better than top-of-the-line steel frames such as those made with Reynolds or Columbus tubing. The expensive frames are lighter, but craftsmanship with these new materials is still in its infancy. You can save a lot of money by choosing a steel frame and still feel confident you have a top-flight bicycle.

There are many technical criteria for judging frames, but the most im-portant standards are simple: is it strong and is it straight? To find out, ask the dealer for a test-ride of the bike. First, just ride around in a trafficless area to see how the bicycle feels. Is the frame responsive? That is, when you pedal, does the bike seem to accelerate eagerly? Or does the bike feel "soft"? That is, as if the frame were soaking up your energy instead of transmitting it to the rear wheel? If it feels soft, it probably is in fact soaking up your energy because the tubes have been put together sloppily, and the frame is bending under your power.

The best test for straightness is a classic one. Ride the bike with no hands on the handlebars. Does the bike go straight without your guidance? It should.

Should the dealer deny you a test-ride—and many will—another test for frame alignment is simply to roll the bike through a puddle of water or a patch of dirt. A straight bike will leave one narrow track—the rear tire will follow the same path as the front.

There are many other things experts look for in a frame, but only one of them is discussed here, because it's controversial: the use, or nonuse, of lugs. A *lug* is a steel sleeve that the tubes fit into at the joints of the frame. This extra metal adds strength at the joint. It also looks neater because it hides the actual welding or soldering tracks underneath. Many books and articles in recent years have argued that lugs are a sign of quality.

This is not necessarily true. Most good bikes do have lugs at the joints. But not all. And an absence of lugs is common on very cheap bikes. But not always. What's more important is how the tubes were joined. Cheaper bikes are generally welded at high temperatures. High temperatures weaken the

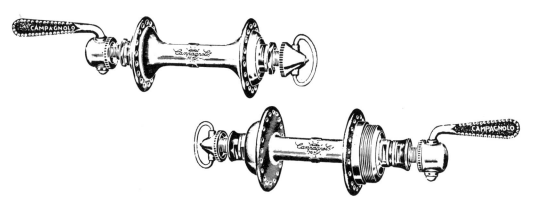

Apart from their convenience, quick-release hubs have the additional benefit of helping to discourage bike theft: if you simply remove your front wheel when you lock up your bike, only the more daring thieves will try to steal the unrideable machine.

metal. Good bikes are brazed or soldered at low temperatures. However, if a bicycle is without lugs, it doesn't mean it was high-temperature welded. Many custom-frame builders don't use lugs because they feel their work is so flawless that lugs are mere window dressing. One builder says that he distrusts lugs because they can be used to hide a multitude of sins such as badly cut tubes or sloppy brazing. And some good mass manufacturers such as Schwinn of the United States and DBS of Norway don't use lugs on many of their bicycles.

So, although it's interesting to see if a bike has lugs or not, it's no certain indication of the bike's quality.

A final piece of frame advice: Generally, bike builders put good components on good frames, medium components on medium frames, and so on. However, it's not uncommon to be faced with two bicycles: one with a mediocre frame but tantalizing components and the other having a good frame but with unexciting parts. Hard as it will be, choose the latter. You'll have a better basic bike, and you can always upgrade the gears, brakes, and other components later. Should you choose the inferior-framed bike, how-ever, there's nothing you can do to upgrade that inferior frame.

Wheels

Although handling and responsiveness depend on the bike frame, sheer speed and ease of pedaling may be more affected by the type of wheels you have. Many racing coaches tell their cost-conscious athletes to put their money into their wheels and skimp, if they have to, on the other parts. Racers are fond of saying, "An ounce on the wheel is worth two on the frame" because rotating mass is the key to acceleration.

There are four things to consider about wheels: the hubs, spokes, rims, and—most important—tires.

You judge a hub by its weight, its smoothness, and convenience. Most hubs are steel, but if you pay more money you can get aluminum alloy ones. The Italian company Campagnolo set the standards in hubs for many years, but there are many, many good hubs on the market today.

Smoothness means how friction-free the axle spins in the hub's ball bearings. Spin the front wheel on any bike you're considering. How smoothly and how long does it spin? Spin the front wheels of other bikes in the store for comparison. Put your ear close to the hub while the wheel is revolving. The less noise you hear the better.

The traditional test for wheels is called the 3 o'clock drop. Position the wheel with the air valve at the 3 o'clock spot with the wheel off the ground so that it can revolve freely. Theoretically, if the wheel is well balanced and adjusted, the mere weight of the valve should make the wheel rotate at least a quarter of a revolution until the valve is at 6 o'clock. This is generally a good test, but it may only mean that the bike has very heavy air valves.

A nice feature to look for in a hub is a quick-release mechanism. Instead of bolts that you must loosen with a wrench to get the wheel off, with a *quick-release mechanism* you simply pull a lever down on one side of the hub and the wheel falls out of the fork blades. This is very convenient when you have a flat tire or have to break down the bike for shipping or storage.

Some very good hubs, usually available only by special order, are permanently sealed. The ball bearings in most hubs are not sealed, and grit, dirt, and moisture get inside and displace the lubricating grease. This means you must overhaul the hubs every year or so to keep them spinning smoothly. This involves taking them apart, wiping out all the grease, and repacking the bearings in new lubricant. *Permanently sealed hubs* need never be overhauled or adjusted.

The problem with permanently sealed hubs is that they're specialty items available only to those buying custom bicycles, where every part can be specified. This situation may be changing, however. At this writing, at least one brand of moderately priced bicycle, Viscount, comes equipped with sealed-bearing hubs. We hope that this is a harbinger of things to come and that soon unsealed bearings will be the exception rather than the rule.

Another fine point: Hubs are either high, or large-flange or low, or small-flange. The *flange* is the holed-lip around the outside of the hub. The holes are for the spokes. Large flanges are about 1 inch (2½ centimeters) in

Check out a bike's rims if you prefer clincher tires to sew-ups, or vice-versa—clincher rims (left) will only accommodate clincher tires, *and tubular rims (right) will only accommodate lighter-weight and faster sew-up tires.*

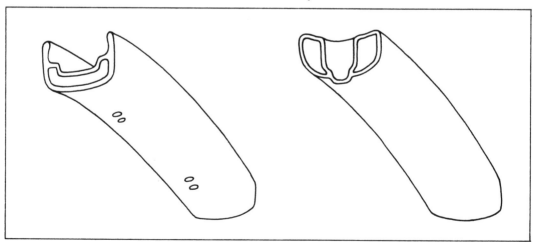

radius, while low flanges are about ⅜ inch (1 centimeter). High flanges are generally advertised as a special feature, as if they were better. They're not. They make the wheel stiffer and therefore perhaps a bit faster over smooth surfaces. Track-racing bicycles or bicycles to be raced over short distances usually have high flanges. However, low flanges allow for longer spokes to absorb road shock and therefore are better over longer distances or rough terrain.

Spokes are too fine an item to worry about. But if you plan to spend a great deal of money you should get *double-butted spokes*, that is, spokes that are thicker at the ends than at the middle for extra strength where it's needed.

Rims are important, but not so much for themselves as for the fact that they will determine what kind of tires you will be limited to. *Clincher*, or *high pressure*, *rims* are for standard clincher tires. *Clincher tires* are open along one edge so that an inner tube can be slipped inside (basically, clincher tires are just like ordinary car tires). Clincher rims must have a lip along either edge that the tire beads can "clinch" to. *Tubular*, or *sprint*, *rims* have no lip, just a smooth, curved surface. This is because *tubular*, or *sew-up*, *tires* are round and totally sealed, with the inner tube sewn up inside. Sew-up tires are glued, taped, or shellacked to the smooth edge of the rim.

Most bikes have clincher rims; tubular rims are found on high-priced models. In a very few cases, you may be offered a choice.

You cannot put clincher tires on your tubular rims or vice versa. You'll have to get entirely new wheels, or at least new rims (which involves taking apart and rebuilding the wheel, an expensive proposition). So the real choice, then, is deciding on the kind of tire you want, which is what makes the tire the most important part of the wheel.

Chester Kyle, professor of mechanical engineering at California State University at Long Beach and one of the founders of the Human-Powered Speed Championships, did his pioneering work with bicycles on tires.

Clincher tires fit on clincher rims (left) and are less expensive and easier to repair than the sew-up tires used on tubular rims (right); but sew-ups are lighter and able to take more pressure, making them much faster to ride and a favorite of racers.

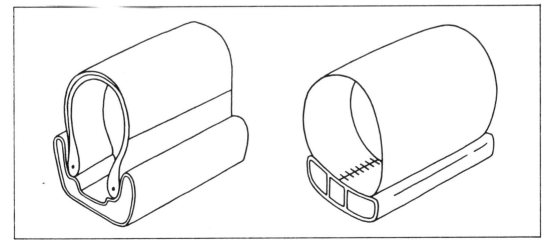

He discovered years ago that by taking the sew-up tires and wheels off an expensive 24-pound (11-kilogram) Le-Jeune bicycle and putting them on a moderately priced 31-pound (14-kilogram) Czechoslovakian Rapido, the latter bike would roll almost as fast as the LeJeune.

Obviously, this points out the importance tires make. In the above instance, the LeJeune tires were high-pressure sew-ups; the Rapido had low-pressure clinchers (with its own tires in place, the Rapido lost the coasting contest to the LeJeune by a considerably wide margin).

Sew-ups are generally faster because they're thinner, thus generating less friction; lighter, and therefore faster accelerating; and—most important—hold more air pressure, making them harder and less friction-producing. A good sew-up tire can hold 100 to 120 pounds per square inch (psi). Standard clinchers hold only 70 psi. But the problem with sew-ups is that they puncture and go flat so easily. And they're just awful to repair. You have to take out all the stitching, patch the tube inside, then resew them. Even then they tend not to patch well. What this means is that, while already higher-priced to begin with, sew-up tires will cost you even more because of their short lifetime. (On the plus side, if you're in a hurry, it's much easier to change a flat sew-up. You simply strip it off the rim and slap on a whole new tire, which, because of lightness and foldability, can be strapped right under the saddle. This is one of the reasons they're a must for racers, who don't have time to patch a standard tire in the middle of a race.)

So, for most people, clincher tires are actually the better choice because they produce fewer flat tires and are much cheaper in the long run. For the racer or the real fanatic, sew-ups are mandatory because of the extra speed they give. And they are a delight to ride. The acceleration and nimbleness sew-ups offer must be experienced to be understood.

Within the sew-up family, there is a wide range of weights and prices. Sew-ups start at about 4 ounces (110 grams), for track racing, and go up to 16 ounces (450 grams) or more. For the average recreational rider, about 10 or 11 ounces (about 300 grams) is about right. Some cyclists who get discouraged over the many flats they get with sew-ups use heavier and heavier models. That doesn't really make sense because of the new lighter-weight clinchers available (which will be discussed shortly). If you decide on sew-ups, decide also to put up with the problems and the expense. Sew-ups are made from cotton and other fibers, but the best are made with silk, which gives a responsive, flexible ride. Silk is very light, but also very tough—and very expensive. The best tire we have ever used for touring is Clement's Campionato del Mondo. It weighs about 10 ounces (280 grams), can be inflated to 115 psi and is quite puncture-resistant. It also costs about the same as 3 or 4 clinchers.

Most of you will be riding on clincher tires, but that doesn't mean you're doomed to mediocrity. The trick is to get tires with the highest possible pressure rating. Usually the maximum allowable pressure is stamped on the side of the tire. Cheap bikes will have 55 psi tires. Don't accept these. Seventy psi is the lowest you should ride on.

And now you can buy clincher tires with very high pressure—85, 95, sometimes even 100 psi—and with a narrow profile as well. This type of tire is almost as hard and thin as a sew-up but has more puncture-resistance and an easily repairable inner tube. This is probably the best innovation the bike industry has come up with in the past decade. The new high-pressure clinchers are available in a number of brands. We highly recommend you try to get some if you like easy pedaling.

Gear Shifters and Gears

Most new riders become obsessed with *derailleurs*, or gear shifters. And it's true, without the derailleur to shift the chain from sprocket to sprocket, you couldn't build a 10-speed, and they are indeed fascinating mechanisms. But we're not going to describe them at length here (see instead pp. 118). Suffice it to say that we've found the metal—steel or aluminum alloy—models to endure longer than the plastic kind. Campagnolo's top-line derailleur is still the standard for the industry. Unfortunately, a pair of Campagnolo derailleurs bought separately are very expensive. The Japanese shifters—Sun Tour and Shimano—are quite adequate and much, much cheaper. Assuming you have limited funds, putting your money into a better frame and wheels makes better sense than spending it on a fancy derailleur.

Oddly enough, the very same people who will talk for hours comparing different brands of derailleurs often ignore a much more crucial matter: the gear ratios a bike offers. Technically speaking, a *gear ratio* is stated in numbers like 2:1 or 3:4:1. But in the bike world, the term *gear values* is used and these are stated in inches or centimeters. A very high gear, for instance, would be 110 inches; a typical low gear would be 40 inches. The way these values are calculated is complicated; all you have to know is that the higher the number, the higher the gear, the farther you go with each

It has been said that the only thing Campagnolo parts can be criticized for is their price—they're expensive! There are two consolations: even used they will probably be worth more than you paid, and they will outlast almost any other brand.

revolution of the pedals, and the harder it is to pedal.

A 10-speed, of course, will have ten of these gear values. One popular 10-speed offers a range from 39 to 104 inches. That is a typical range, but not a very good one. The highest gear is one you'll rarely need, and the lowest is not low enough. Always ask the dealer what the gear range is, and pay particular attention to that lowest gear. Try to get a low gear around 34 or 35 inches—lower still, if possible, but it's rare to find anything under 34. If you find a bike that's perfect in every respect except its low gear is not low enough, ask the dealer to change the gearing. This can be done by changing the freewheel cluster on the back wheel. If the dealer won't, or can't, do this, go to another bike store. You won't regret it when riding steep hills. (And we've never found a bike with too low a low gear.) However, if a dealer does agree to make the change, it's reasonable for the dealer to charge you for this service.

There are, of course, nine other gears, and there are elaborate theories on how those gear values should be spaced out. But, for most cyclists, that is too fine a point.

Brakes

Always perform this test on a new bike: Squeeze both brake levers closed as if you were making a panic stop. Do it hard, with all your strength. If the brakes are weak or improperly assembled, this action will pop the cable

ends right out of the housings. This could greatly offend the bike store owner. If so, return the indignation. If you had bought the bicycle and needed to make a panic stop on the road, you would have ended in the hospital.

There are two types of hand brakes generally found on 10-speeds: side-pulls and center-pulls. With *side-pull brakes*, the cable pulls the calipers together from one side only. With *center-pull brakes*, the cable pulls the calipers together from the center with a carrier cable transmitting the force equally to each of the caliper arms. Many books and articles written in recent years say that center-pulls are superior. This is not really true. It's much more complicated than that.

Side-pull brakes need less material and fewer parts. This is why makers of cheap bikes like them. But they can be made more cheaply. Side-pull brakes, however, do have the potential of stop-

Side-pull brakes (left) have two design disadvantages with respect to center-pull brakes (right): a single pivot creates all the *action and thus force is frequently unevenly applied. Still, the best of the side-pulls are superior to center-pulls.*

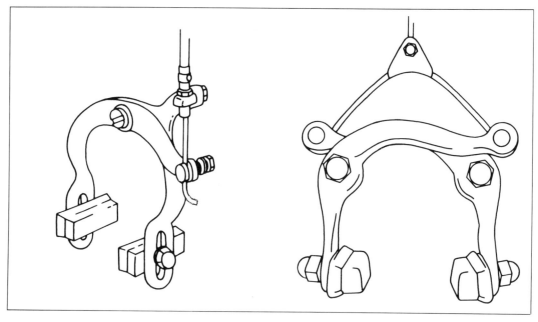

ping a bike faster than center-pulls because a single cable pulling both caliper arms together simultaneously is faster than using two different cables as in center-pulls. This is why makers of very high-quality bikes also like side-pulls. But getting the simple side-pull design to work consistently requires good materials and skilled workmanship. Therefore, side-pulls can be either very cheap or very expensive. And center-pulls fall in the middle.

Center-pulls are usually a safe choice. If a bike has side-pulls, it might be wonderful or terrible. To test side-pulls, squeeze the brake handles a few times and watch the actual brake pads hit the rim of the wheel. Does one pad always end up closer to the wheel than the other after you release the lever? If it does, it's the sign of a side-pull brake that isn't centering properly, and it should be avoided.

Handlebars and Stems

The important decision here is whether you want flat or dropped handlebars. The dropped, so-called racing handlebars, are probably the best choice if you plan to ride any distance. They offer more hand positions, so your fingers don't get tired over long journeys. By keeping you low, dropped handlebars help cut down wind resistance. They divide your body weight more evenly between the handlebars and saddle (which means your behind will get less pressure). And the dropped-down position lets you make better use of your back and shoulder muscles to offset your pedaling and usually improves your breathing because it's easier for your chest and lungs to expand.

So there's a good case for dropped handlebars. In fact, many experts say anything else is folly. But for city traffic, where you should be looking around all the time, and will be getting off and on the bike frequently, the old flat-style handlebars are practical and comfortable.

Like most components, handlebars come in either steel or aluminum alloy, the latter being more expensive and lighter. On very expensive track-racing bicycles the handlebars are usually steel because track cyclists exert tremendous pressure during sprints that would bend the alloy bars.

Make sure the handlebars are taped. Cloth or rubberized tape is comfortable, the plastic tape less so. The open ends of the handlebars should have plugs in them; an unplugged handlebar can slash you badly.

Take a close look at the *stem*—the piece of metal that comes up from the head tube, makes a right-angle turn and sticks out to hold the handlebar. You must check the stem for length. Oddly enough, manufacturers don't pay much attention to this detail, and stems are often out of proportion. You can find a 24-inch (60-centimeter) bike with, say, a 2½-inch (6-centimeter) stem or 20-inch (50-centimeter) bikes with 4-inch (10-centimeter) stems.

How long should a stem be? It depends on the length of your arms, so do the forearm stretch test. First, set the saddle so that it's even with the top of the stem. Place your elbow at the tip of the saddle, and stretch your forearm straight forward. The ends of your fingertips should reach the back edge of the handlebar at the end of the stem. If you can't reach it, the stem's too long. If you over-reach it, it's too short.

In the past most stems were tightened with a normal protruding bolt that stuck out of the top, and very expensive stems featured a recessed

Allen nut. But this is no longer a clue to quality. Many manufacturers have switched to Allen nuts to give their stems a quasi-expensive look.

Cranks and Chainrings

The *cranks* are the arms that the pedals are attached to, and the *chainrings*, or *chainwheels*, are attached to the cranks. Usually, this whole assembly is made by the same manufacturer for compatibility.

There are three kinds of cranks: one-piece, cottered, and cotterless. The *one-piece crank* is usually found on cheaper bikes as the two cranks and the axle that connects them are molded from the same piece of steel. This is a heavy kind of crank, and if it breaks the whole thing has to be replaced. But one-piece cranks aren't necessarily bad, and some European companies use them on good 10-speeds. After all, the simplicity of the device leaves little to go wrong. But a one-piece crank may be a warning that the rest of the bike may not be so

good as this is a cheaper type of component. If everything else on the bicycle is fine, however, it is not a serious drawback.

Cottered steel cranks are more common in medium-priced bicycles. *Cottered cranks* are connected to the axle, or spindle, with cotter pins. These can break or fall out, and that can be a problem, though not a frequent one.

Cotterless cranks are invariably made of aluminum and are expensive. They have no cotter pin to break. A special bolt secures the cranks to the axle. You will need a special cotterless crank tool to tighten or loosen these cranks (and usually each brand requires a different tool). Cotterless cranks are light, strong, and reasonably trouble free, but on long trips you'll need to carry that tool with you.

To test cottered and cotterless cranks for workmanship, grab the pedals, one in each hand. Now jerk them back and forth to make sure that the cranks are moving together

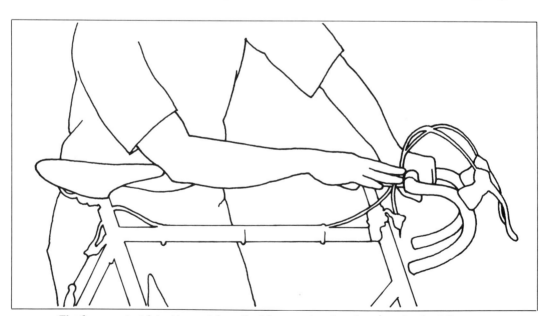

The forearm stretch test is a quick method for determining whether your bike's stem is the right length for you. This is no trivial detail: *stem length can make the difference between comfortable and uncomfortable riding especially over long distances.*

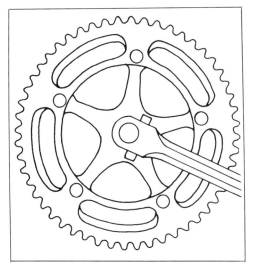

Cottered cranks are adequate for most bike riders. But check that the pins haven't worn and fallen out. Riding the bike without pins can destroy the cranks.

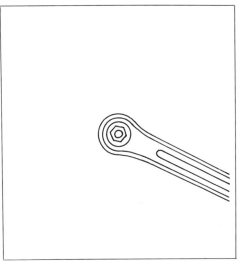

Cotterless cranks are extremely strong, durable, and trouble-free. However, they should be tightened occasionally to ensure they are seated properly.

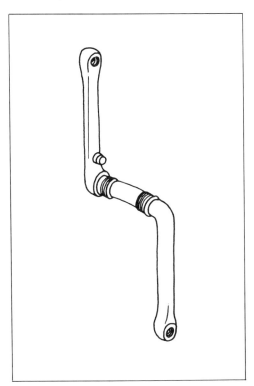

One-piece cranks are frequently used on children's bikes and are usually heavier than cottered cranks, but they can be functional and lasting components provided the bike manufacturer uses good components for the rest of the bicycle.

and not clanking around loosely on the spindle. One-piece cranks are, of course, free of such problems.

Saddle

Last, but certainly not least, is the saddle. In fact, this item rates in importance above derailleurs, handlebars, and cranks. The best bike in the world is no good if you're too sore to ride it.

The biggest mistake people make is to buy any padded saddle. Don't be fooled by padding. Check underneath the saddle to see what the base is made of. If it's metal, it's no good. After a while the padding mats down, spreads to the sides, and you're left sitting on the steel base. Padded saddles with nylon or plastic bases are okay. An even safer bet is a leather saddle, which may feel hard at first but softens after a few hundred miles to custom-fit your bottom. (Nylon or plastic won't do this.) A few companies have sprung up lately that specialize in super-comfortable, but expensive, saddles. Avocet and Cool Gear are two of them.

3-SPEED AND 1-SPEED BICYCLES

Before you put down the money for that new 10-speed, simply ask yourself, "Do I really need this?" Will you go for 50-mile trips? Will you be on the road for more than one day at a time? Or will you be spending more time pedaling across town?

Ten-speeds do take some care and maintenance, and if you're not going any distance, they just aren't worth it. The 3-speed's shift mechanism is reasonably carefree, and it has the advantage of being inside the rear hub where no one can kick it. With the emphasis on 10-speeds, 3-speeds have also become good value for money.

Less glamorous than the 5- and 10-speeds, the sturdy 3-speed bike is far more practical for the sort of heavy wear you are likely to experience in towns and in general short-distance riding. Its no-nonsense design (which has changed little in over 20 years) sacrifices lightness and speed for durability and practicality. This makes it a very good buy secondhand —vintage models 20 years old and more can still give sterling service.

As for 1-speeds, they're still good for kids, newspaper deliveries, or as beach bikes—anywhere terrain is bad and bumpy. They're virtually indestructible. And who's going to steal one?

Another kind of 1-speed is the track bike, or fixed-wheel bicycle. Unlike the coaster-brake bike, however, it has no brakes and is meant for racing on a

The 3-speed bike is a sensible and useful idea, terrific for short hops around town. Unfortunately, the upper limit to their quality is only moderate-to-good. Still, it remains the most popular kind of bicycle in Europe.

banked oval track. You cannot coast on this bicycle as it has no freewheel. As long as the bike is rolling, you have to keep your feet rotating with the pedals. This makes it difficult to get off. These are fun bikes to ride, though, once you get the hang of them.

Track bikes are not for everyone, however. They are designed for a specific purpose—racing under strictly controlled conditions on smooth, banked tracks (see Chapter 6). They have neither the versatility of the 10-speed nor the durability of the 3-speed. In the pursuit of lightness they are stripped of all unnecessary accessories, from pump clips to brakes. Yet they are not cheap: only the lightest and strongest components are used, and a good track bike can easily cost as much as the best 10-speeds.

But having said this, the appeal of a track bike lies not just in its novelty or the purity of its simple elegant lines. A track bike is designed for high responsiveness and precise handling over the short distances of track races. Although initially difficult to master, a fixed wheel will give you closer control over speed and over maneuverability. The sharp angles of a track frame and its rigid construction, which make it an uncomfortable ride over long distances, also give it a sharp, almost twitchy responsiveness once you are in the saddle. This, of course, may not be to your liking, but there is no denying that for the experienced rider a track bike has a very special appeal even off the track.

The fixed-wheel bicycle has no brakes and is designed to be ridden at high speeds around a bicycle track—obviously, it's not the bike for anyone who wants basic street transportation.

MIXTES AND FOLDERS

Another bicycle to consider is the mixte. This is a hybrid between a man's- and a woman's-style bike. A man's bike has a straight top tube for strength. A woman's bike has a U-shaped tube in its place, traditionally to allow the wearing of a full skirt. Few women want to wear skirts anymore while cycling, yet some of them still harbor fears of that top tube acquired from learning to ride on the so-called girl's bike. The mixte is a compromise. It has no top tube but no U-shaped tube either. Instead, it has two tubes running in tandem from the head tube all the way to the rear, where they are joined with the seat and chain stays. The mixte is stronger than a traditional woman's bike and less threatening than a man's.

The folding bicycle is a vehicle in turmoil these days. The very convenient, light models are quite expensive. The more affordable ones are heavy, well over 30 pounds (13 kilograms), and despite being foldable (usually with a hinge in the middle of the frame) are hardly convenient to carry to an upstairs apartment or office. But they are maneuverable in city traffic, thanks to their small wheels and low center of gravity. The folding bike is one of those things that's nice to have around as a second bicycle for strictly local use, but it's not something that you'd buy as your primary form of transportation. And the turmoil surrounds the fact that folding bikes are finding it harder and harder to meet government safety standards in America.

The mixte, or unisex, bicycle is a compromise choice for women who want a bike better than the usual range of women's bikes but don't want to go all the way to men's bikes. These bikes should be judged on the same criteria as regular 10-speeds.

Fold-up bikes can be convenient to store, but they also force you to choose between the very heavy and the very expensive. They can be useful as second bikes, however, and frequently come with lots of "extras" that make them even more useable.

Chapter 2

RIDING FOR FITNESS AND HEALTH

Bicycling falls into that special group of exercises known as *aerobic*, or oxygen-using, exercises. Very simply, these type of exercises give your body a total going-over by not only working the muscles in your arms, legs, and torso but working vital inner muscles, namely your heart and diaphragm, as well. They are called aerobic exercises because they make your body become more efficient in absorbing and using that most vital of all gases, oxygen.

Sports such as swimming, running, cross-country skiing, and bicycling are considered aerobic because they force your body to take in and use more oxygen. Other sports such a golf, weight lifting, or horseback riding, don't. While they may build up strength in certain parts of your body, they don't do very much for other aspects of fitness: physical endurance and stamina—the ability of your body to work hard without strain over a period of time.

By working your body during your aerobic exercise sessions, you're making it stronger, tougher, and healthier. But does it really matter if you choose an aerobic exercise like bicycling over another like calesthenics or weight lifting?

THE PHYSICAL BENEFITS OF AEROBICS

If you want to increase the odds of living a long, healthy life, choosing an aerobic exercise does matter. In one elaborate study done over a period of 10 years, a doctor kept careful track of the health and the exercise habits of 17,000 men, even itemizing how many steps they climbed per day. The doctor found that those who stayed most consistently healthy were those who spent anywhere from 2½ to 3 hours per week doing some kind of aerobic exercise.

The reason those people stayed consistently healthy is that a habit of exercise is a form of insurance against one of the great killers of modern times, heart disease. Doctors know, for example, that the more a muscle is used, the stronger it becomes. And that's what the heart is—a muscle, one that pumps blood. The more you exercise, the harder your heart has to work to keep the blood circulating.

Your body needs that blood for a variety of reasons: to carry nutrients, to fight infection, to remove wastes, and to carry oxygen. Your red blood cells have in them a pigment called hemoglobin that absorbs oxygen from your lungs and carries it off to wherever you need it. Your muscles need this oxygen to continue working at peak efficiency.

Most of your muscles' fuel is either in the form of a natural sugar called glycogen or in the form of body fat. A muscle can't convert either of these fuels into energy without oxygen. That's why it's so important that your circulatory system be able to deliver as much blood as possible where oxygen is needed the most. (In the case of bicycling, those muscles would be the ones in the legs.) So the harder the muscles work, the more blood they need to burn the body's fuel. And the more blood needed, the harder the heart has to work as well. Fortunately, like any muscle that gets used a lot, the heart gets stronger. As a result, it can do the same amount of work as before with less effort.

Once you've been bicycling a while you may find that your pulse rate has changed, actually slowed down. Suppose you have the average pulse rate of about 72 beats per minute. As your heart gets more accustomed to your exercising, you might see your pulse drop to 60 or even 50 beats per minute. What this means is that it is pumping out the same amount of blood with fewer beats.

It's easy to find your pulse's resting rate. Simply get a watch with a sweep hand and press your finger lightly on the artery near the base of the jaw or rest your index and middle finger at the pulse point on the inside of your wrist and count your pulse for a full minute. If you're average, you'll find that it is somewhere around the low 70s. If you've already been exercising a while, you might find it's below that. If it's been a while since you've done any kind of exercise, on the other hand, you may find it higher than the low to mid-70s. In fact, if it happens to be over 80 beats per minute, maybe it's time to think seriously about starting some kind of exercise.

In addition to becoming a stronger muscle, a bicyclist's heart becomes more efficient in other ways. Doctors have also found that as you exercise more, the network of blood vessels actually increases in response to the new demand for more blood. Doctors have found, for example, that the coronary arteries that supply blood to your heart actually get larger, keeping your heart muscle fueled better and making it less susceptible to heart problems. As the size and number of blood vessels increase, it becomes less difficult to keep blood circulating. You have the same amount of blood flowing through more vessels, easing the amount of a push your heart has to give to get the blood to where it's needed.

Aerobic exercises also improve the quality of your blood. For one thing, it becomes more efficient at absorbing and carrying oxygen. The reason for this is that the more you exercise, the more the volume of your blood supply increases. You actually have more of those hemoglobin-carrying red blood cells. And since it is the hemoglobin that's responsible for getting the oxygen from your lungs to your muscle tissue, that means you have more oxygen ready to use.

Your blood also improves in another way: The level of certain natural body fats, called triglycerides, drops. This is an added bonus, especially when you realize that these fats have been implicated in heart attacks. What happens in a body with too many triglycerides is that they pile up and clog the bloodstream. When you exercise, this is less likely to happen.

If you're faithful to your exercise regimen, you'll find that you'll be getting slimmer as well. What happens is that your body burns the excess fat and builds up more muscle. Depending on how fast and hard you bicycle, for example, you can burn anywhere from 200 to over 500 calories per hour. (See chart shown below.) And, if you eat the same amount of food now as before you started bicycling, the excess fat will melt away quickly. In general it's estimated that to lose one pound or kilogram of fat, you have to burn about 3,500 or 7,000 calories over and above your daily intake.

Other less obvious benefits of an aerobic exercise like bicycling include its effect on your digestive system. People with stomach problems such as ulcers have noticed that their ailments lessen or even clear up after exercising. Why this is no one knows for sure, but one guess is that exercise has a relaxing, antistress effect, making a person less susceptible to pressure. Also the well-exercised body seems to produce less gastric acid while digesting food, a bonus for the ulcer-prone person. Finally, the whole process of digesting food seems to speed up and become more efficient. The reason for this seems to be that exercising speeds up the contractions of the intestines as they move food and digested waste through the system.

BICYCLING AND YOUR MIND

More and more, medical experts of all kinds are beginning to realize that getting in the habit of doing an invigorating exercise is good for the brain as well as the body. Just on a very basic level, an aerobic exercise like bicycling is excellent for what could be called brain fitness. As a result of the improvement in circulation from exercising, the brain gets better supplied with oxygen and other nutrients. This explains why after a particularly

A BICYCLIST'S CALORIE CHART

CYCLING SPEED	CALORIES CONSUMED
6 mph. (10 kmph)	250 Calories/hour
8 mph. (13 kmph)	330 Calories/hour
10 mph. (16 kmph)	450 Calories/hour
12 mph. (19 kmph)	560 Calories/hour

Note: These figures refer to the average cycling speed over reasonably flat terrain. If there are a lot of uphill climbs, of course, you'll consume more calories. (And conversely, the more downhill runs you have, the fewer the calories consumed.)

hard ride your body might feel tired but your mind may feel more alert than ever before. That increased circulation of blood you're sending to your brain can really perk it up.

Once you start bicycling routinely you may also find that you feel more relaxed, more self-confident as your body fitness improves.

Some psychiatrists have found that a good aerobic exercise, such as bicycling, running, or swimming, can also be helpful in treating one of the most common of mental problems, that is, depression.

Instead of having mildly depressed patients come in for a session of analysis, these pyschiatrists are recommending that they exercise instead. This gets their patients' minds off their problems, helps lift their depression and, some researchers believe, may even work biochemically to relieve mild depression. Exercise seems to raise the amount of an important chemical called norepinephrine in the system. Important for shuttling messages between brain cells, norepinephrine, doctors suspect, is also a natural antidepressant. They have found that depressed people tend to have low levels of norepinephrine in their bloodstream and that their depression lessens as the amount of this chemical increases.

Other doctors have found that just 15 minutes of exercise a day can release some of the tension shut up in your body. A researcher from the University of California using delicate electrical measurements of muscle tension found that his nervous patients were able to reduce their natural tension levels by as much as 75 percent after exercising for a quarter hour every day.

Another fringe benefit of taking up exercise like bicycling is its effect on your sleep. People who have complained about insomnia find that they no longer have that problem once they make exercise a habit. After you've been bicycling a while, you'll probably find you will sleep more soundly than ever before and feel more refreshed than ever when you wake in the morning. Because exercise seems to relieve tension and depression, two causes of insomnia, it also makes a good sleeping medicine.

BICYCLING AND LONGEVITY

It's a fact of life that as people get older, they lose ground physically. Starting about the age of 20, we pass our physical peak, and some of our natural resilience and stamina start to fade. After testing hundreds of people, a team of Swedish researchers found that the body's aerobic capacity, that is, its ability to absorb and use oxygen, declines at the average rate of slightly less than 1 percent—0.8 percent to be exact—each year. If, for the sake of an example, you're operating at 100 percent aerobic capacity at age 20, by the time you reach 30 (assuming you're the average person) your body can work at only 89 percent of its former capacity. By age 40, that has dropped to 79 percent. It's not an even falloff—it starts quickly in the younger years and slows as you get older—but it does happen at a fairly predictable rate.

In addition to losing some of its natural stamina, a body that is unexercised is even more susceptible to some of the enemies of good health. You can become prone to getting overweight and have the health problems (high blood pressure, heart disease) that come with that condition. If you have other bad habits—such as drinking too much or smoking—you can further cut into your natural longevity.

Some of these problems can be corrected with diet—cutting down on fats and alcohol—and others, such as smoking, can be eliminated. What's more, you can speed up your return to good health and better prospects for a longer life by getting on your bike and riding. By cultivating the habit of exercise, you can not only slow some of the effects of aging but even reverse them somewhat.

Physical fitness experts have found that people of any age, even those well into their 70s, who followed a program of exercise 3 hours per week actually had the physical profiles of someone 20 or even 30 years younger. Their weight remained stable. Their maximum heart rates—the pulse of the heart when working the hardest—actually declined, and even their lung capacities increased. They were physically younger.

Besides these obvious benefits of physical fitness, there are more subtle ones as well. People who exercise regularly also seem to be able to keep their appetites under control, so they don't go on eating binges, as they might have in the past. They find their craving for alcohol lessens. Some even find it easier to give up smoking.

GUIDELINES FOR DEVELOPING FITNESS

To attain a healthy level of fitness, you have to bicycle, or do some kind of aerobic exercise, hard at least 1½ hours each week. Just how hard is "hard" training? According to fitness specialists, during your exercise time your body should be working at between 60 and 80 percent of your maximum heart rate, basically the fastest your heart can beat and pump blood to your body. You don't know what your maximum heart beat is? Here's a simple formula you can use to find out: Subtract your age from 220. For example, if you're 25 years old, your maximum heart rate is 195. This means that when you bicycle for fitness, your heart should be beating at roughly 60 percent of that, 117 beats per minute or if you are extremely athletic, 80 percent—roughly 150 beats per minute. During that period of exercise, you're stretching your body's heart-and-circulation, or cardiovascular, fitness to new and healthier limits.

According to Dr. Per-Olof Astrand, Chairman of the Department of Physiology at the Karolinska Institute in Stockholm, the ideal exercise week should be 5 hours a week and include 1 hour of light exercise—walking, for example—every day and three intense half-hour exercise sessions as well. If you don't see yourself doing 5 hours of routine exercise a week (and not many people do), try to get in a total of at least 3 hours a week total. Start with 1½ hours a week and gradually work your way up.

Once you've begun your exercise program, don't make the mistake of assuming that the level of fitness you get from it is permanent, or even very long lasting. After just a couple of weeks without exercise, your fitness will deteriorate. And in as little as 3 to 4 weeks of total inertia, you can slide back to your pre-exercise level of non-fitness. So whatever you do, don't drop your fitness regimen and assume you have somehow been permanently immunized against getting out of shape. Cycling should not be an occasional treatment for being out of shape; it should become a part of your life.

Stretching, Warm-ups, and Cool-downs

Steady exercise tightens and actually shortens muscle fibers. Muscles not only become stronger, but they also become subject to strain and injury if you don't loosen them up before going for a ride. That's why you should warm up for each cycling session with a few stretching exercises to loosen up your muscles, particularly those in the leg. Always take the time to do at least one of the hamstring and calf-muscle exercises, described in the exercise section at the end of this chapter, before and after a ride. Your legs will feel looser and more relaxed as a result.

Warming up the rest of your body before you head out riding is just as important as warming up your legs. You wouldn't start up and drive a car at top speed on an ice-cold morning, so why do that to your body? It needs time to get ready. As part of your prebicycling warm-up, do the stretching exercises and one short series of sit-ups or push-ups to get the blood moving a little faster. This is particularly important in cool or cold weather.

Just as important is the tapering off or cooling down part of each exercise session. Take about 5 minutes to do some slow, steady pedaling before you stop completely. Don't be careless and stop dead after a strenuous ride. If you've done that in the past, you probably already know some of the after effects: lightheadedness and dizziness. Some people have even fainted by stopping too suddenly after an exercise session—not a good thing to have happen to you if you happen to be sitting on a bike. The reason this happens is that when you stop, the blood has to pool, or concentrate, in the muscles that have been working the hardest. In the case of bicycling this would be your legs. When you stop suddenly, you don't give your circulatory system time enough to correct this imbalance and the result

is that your brain is blood-starved and you keel over.

Weather

Although people seem to worry about it too much, cold is not as dangerous to exercise in as hot, humid weather. If you're dressed for cold weather (and there's no snow or ice on the roads), you won't have to worry about the cold unless the temperature drops below freezing or the wind-chill factor lowers it to that point. When it gets that cold, it might be a good idea to postpone outdoor riding and do an indoor alternative until things warm up a bit.

When it's hot and humid, as a general rule think twice about exercising outdoors once the temperature climbs into the high 80s Fahrenheit (the high 20s Celsius) and/or the humidity starts rising above 70 percent. The reason is that high temperatures and high humidity put an added strain on your body by forcing your natural thermostat to try to keep yourself cool and exposing you to the risk of heat stroke. If you want to cycle during hot weather, the best way to do it is to ride early in the morning before the day's heat builds up.

Know Your Limits

There's a familiar pattern among some people who start a new sport or exercise. If that sport is cycling, they buy the most expensive bike they can afford; a whole line of accessories to clip, bolt, or otherwise attach to it; and a brand new biker's wardrobe. The very first day they charge out on the roads and pedal their legs off. This procedure lasts two, maybe three days before they can't stand the muscle pain, the stiff, sore legs, and the aches all over their bodies. And in very little time they've hung up the bike or sold it to someone.

What you'll have to do if you want to avoid this fate is start slowly, as mentioned before, and also know what your limits are when you exercise. You already know that when you exercise hard it should be at 60 to 80 percent of your maximum heart rate (220 minus your age), which you can detect in one of these two ways: You can stop, take your pulse for 10 seconds (feel the artery at the base of your jaw) and multiply by six; or if you don't feel like doing that, there is a slightly simpler way. When you are exercising so hard that your breaths are coming out in steady rhythmic sighs, you have hit that maximum level.

There are danger signs to watch for when you pass that level, ones that you should know about. First, if you feel lightheaded, nauseated, dizzy, or severe pains in your chest, stop immediately. You're overdoing it. Another symptom is breathlessness. If you're on the verge of gasping for air, slow down. And if you suspect you are pushing yourself too hard, give yourself a brief follow-up checkup about 10 minutes after your bicycling session. If you are still short of breath and/or your pulse is 100 beats per minute or more, you are probably overdoing it and should cut down on your schedule.

One last word of caution: Before starting any exercise program, have a thorough physical checkup by your doctor, especially if you are over 30 or have done little or no exercising in the past. Your bicycling program is supposed to help you, not harm you, so make sure you're ready to start.

YOUR EXERCISE PROGRAM

What we've outlined here is a basic 6-phase program for the beginner through to the experienced level of bicyclist. Although it's possible to run through this program in 6 weeks, don't make the mistake of trying to force your body to a schedule. The program gets harder as it goes on, and you may hit an exercise plateau where you have to spend a couple of extra weeks doing the same routine before you can move on comfortably to the next phase.

Finally, one last word about riding. Keep a smooth, easy rhythm in your legs as you pedal. Make a conscious effort to set and hold a steady *cadence*, which is the number of times you rotate your pedals each minute, or revolutions per minute (rpm). Try for a cadence of 70 rpm. You should be spinning your feet fairly quickly with a minimum of pushing resistance. Experiment a little until you find the gear that will let you hit and hold that rhythm. (This should be easier with a 10-speed bike.) If 70 rpm is too tiring, start at a slower cadence and work your way up to it. Whatever cycle of pedal speed you settle on, try to maintain it as much as possible.

This is your 6-phase program. The days marked in italics are the ones on which you should ride hard, that is at an intensive enough tempo to get you breathing at a regular "sighing," or maximum pulse, rate. The schedule is for 5 days a week. On Saturday, you have the option of taking a long, steady ride if you want to put your fitness to the test. Again we remind you that these times are not absolute. If you don't feel like riding for 40 minutes one day, don't. Do what feels comfortable. It's more important that you get out and do some riding than you stay home and do nothing at all. Remember, though, that to be beneficial, your exercise rides should total at least 1½ hours per week.

6-PHASE EXERCISE PROGRAM

PHASE 1		*PHASE 2*	
DAY	RIDING TIME	DAY	RIDING TIME
Mon.	20 minutes	*Mon.*	30 Minutes
Tues.	15 minutes (or take day off)	Tues.	15 minutes (or take day off)
Wed.	20 minutes	*Wed.*	30 minutes
Thurs.	15 minutes (or take day off)	Thurs.	15 minutes (or take day off)
Fri.	20 minutes	*Fri.*	30 minutes
Sat.	Day off	Sat.	Optional long ride: 5 to 10 miles (8 to 16 kilometers)

PHASE 3		*PHASE 4*	
DAY	RIDING TIME	DAY	RIDING TIME
Mon.	40 minutes	*Mon.*	50 minutes
Tues.	20 minutes	Tues.	25 minutes
Wed.	40 minutes	*Wed.*	50 minutes
Thurs.	20 minutes	Thurs.	25 minutes
Fri.	40 minutes	*Fri.*	50 minutes
Sat.	Optional long ride: 10 to 15 miles (16 to 24 kilometers)	Sat.	Optional long ride: 20 miles (32 kilometers)

PHASE 5		*PHASE 6*	
DAY	RIDING TIME	DAY	RIDING TIME
Mon.	60 minutes	*Mon.*	70 minutes
Tues.	30 minutes	Tues.	35 minutes
Wed.	60 minutes	*Wed.*	70 minutes
Thurs.	30 minutes	Thurs.	35 minutes
Fri.	60 minutes	*Fri.*	70 minutes
Sat.	Optional ride: 25 to 30 miles (40 to 48 kilometers)	Sat.	Optional ride: 40 to 50 miles (64 to 80 kilometers)

Warming Up

Before every ride, take about 5 minutes to stretch and loosen your muscles, particularly your hamstring muscles (the large muscle at the back of your thigh) and your calf muscles (the muscles on the back of your lower leg). When you first start riding, you may feel some aches and pains in your neck, shoulders, and lower back until your body adjusts. We also have some suggestions for loosening them.

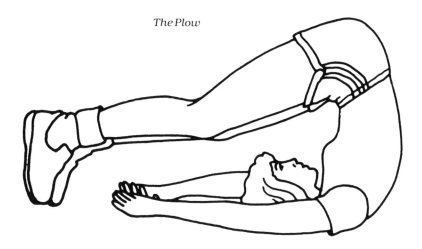

The Plow

Hamstring stretches. Do one of the following exercises before you take a ride and after a ride.

Toe Touches: Put your feet together and keep your legs straight. Bend over and try to touch your toes with your fingertips. It doesn't matter if you do or not. What's important is that you bend down as far as you can. Hold that position for about 10 seconds, and then straighten up. Do this three to five times. Don't bounce as you reach down, but do it in an easy stretching motion.

Sitting Stretch: Sit on the floor with your hands behind your back and your feet together stretched straight out in front of you. Hold your shoulders back, and slowly bend forward as far as you can. Then ease yourself back upright. Do this three to five times.

The Plow: This is a yoga-style exercise that is good for stretching both your hamstrings and lower back muscles. It looks hard but it isn't. Just make sure you pick a soft, carpeted spot on the floor before you do it. Lie on your

Sitting Stretch

back, and keeping your legs together, raise them up and over your head so that you are resting on your shoulders. To exercise, try to reach the ground with your toes. Stretch your legs down as far as you can and hold for a slow count of ten. Do this three to five times.

Calf muscle stretch. Do the standard push-up described below in addition to one hamstring stretch.

Standing Push-up: Stand about 4 feet (1 meter) from a wall with your feet spread comfortably apart. Keep your legs straight, and lean forward making sure both feet are flat on the floor. Steady yourself against the wall with your hands. Now bend your elbows so that your face starts moving slowly toward the wall. Make sure to keep your back straight all the while. When you've leaned forward as far as you think you can, hold that position for a slow count of ten, then straighten up. Do this three to five times.

Optional exercises. If you're feeling a little stiff in some other parts of your body, maybe the following will help. As with the others, do the ones you choose before and after a ride.

Neck exercise: If your bike has dropped handlebars, you may have a stiff neck from looking up while the rest of your body is lowered down over the bike. Try this neck twirl exercise to shake out some of the kinks.

Keep your shoulders steady, and using only your neck muscles, very

Standing Push-up, Step 1   *Standing Push-up, Step 2*

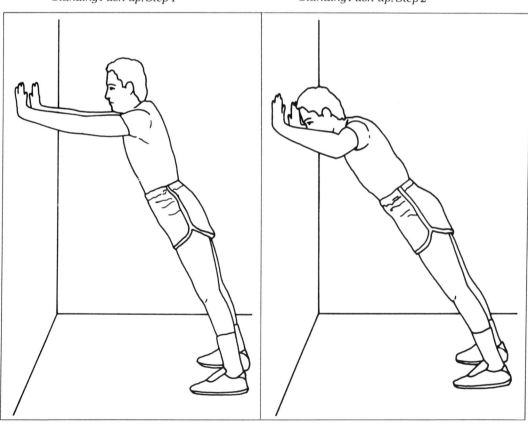

slowly rotate your head from right to left making as wide a circle as possible as you do it. Now do the same equally slowly in the other direction. Take about 15 seconds to do each rotation. Do it a couple of times each way.

Shoulder exercise: This is an easy exercise using very simple equipment —specifically a broomstick. First, let your arms hang down naturally in front of you and hold the broomstick, palms facing in, so that it is horizontal. Now, doing a slow count of ten, raise your arms up and as far back over your head as you can and return them to your starting position. This whole rotation should take about 10 to 15 seconds. Do this three to five times.

Lower back: If your back is bothering you, you could do the plow described earlier or this easy exercise called the pelvic tilt. Lie on your back with your legs bent and your feet comfortably apart. You can put your hands behind your head or straight out to your sides. Now using a concentrated effort, press the small of your back down flat against the floor and squeeze your buttocks together. Hold that pose for 10 seconds. You'll have to raise your hips a few inches or centimeters and press your shoulders down against the floor as you do it. Hold the press position for 10 seconds, and do a series of ten of these.

Strengthening Your Body

You might feel a few weak spots in your body when you start cycling, and you may want to work on them in your spare time. This is easier than you think, and for the most part doesn't require any special equipment.

Here's a series of exercises for different areas of the body that get tired during a ride. The big difference between these and the stretching exercises is that, instead of doing them every day, you do them only three times a week so that your muscles have a chance to build up and recover. The series starts from the neck and works down, offering exercises for your neck, abdomen, lower back, hamstrings, and quadriceps.

Neck power. Often the stiff neck you get in bicycling is the result of neck muscles not being accustomed to holding your head up at a sharp angle for such a long time. You can help it adjust with the following simple exercise, which is basically a variation of the head twirl stretching exercise we described earlier. Move your head slowly in a right-to-left circle, as described in the head twirl movement, taking about 10 seconds to complete the cycle. Only this time as you do it, place your hand against the right side of your head and push continuously against the motion of your head as you swing it around. The idea is to place some resistance against your head and make your neck muscles work a little harder. Press gently at first. Make sure to do the rotation in both directions at least once. Each rotation should take from about 10 to 15 seconds.

Abdominal exercises. While bent over your bike, you place a real strain on your torso muscles, specifically those of your abdomen. All it takes to strengthen your midsection is to do a series of sit-ups to get in shape. The exercise is simple (but not always easy at first). Lie on your back with your knees bent and your feet flat on the floor. Put your hands behind your head, and then try to sit up as far as you can, moving in a slow, steady motion. Don't jerk or throw your body up and forward. (That's cheating and won't do you much physical good anyway.) If you're having trouble keeping your feet down, anchor them under

Sit-up

the edge of your bed or couch. Do as many as you can manage each session, working up to 50.

If you don't find the sit-up comfortable, an alternative exercise is the leg lift and spread. Lie on your back with your arms straight out by your sides. Your legs should be close together and straight. To exercise, slowly raise your legs together until your heels are about 6 inches (15 centimeters) off the floor, then spread them apart like the blades of a pair of scissors, bring them back together again, and slowly lower them. Ideally, you should do three sets of ten repetitions each. If you can't do ten at first, do three sets of whatever number is possible and work your way up to ten.

Lower back. The exercises for the abdomen will help a little in strengthening your lower back as well, but if you want something specifically for that part of your body, you could try this exercise, which we call the semi-cobra exercise (because it vaguely re-

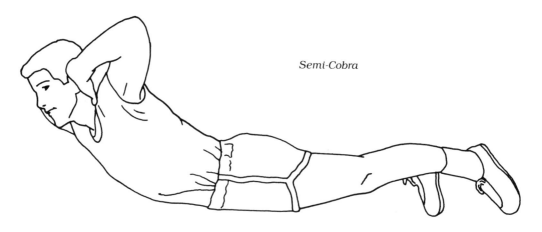

Semi-Cobra

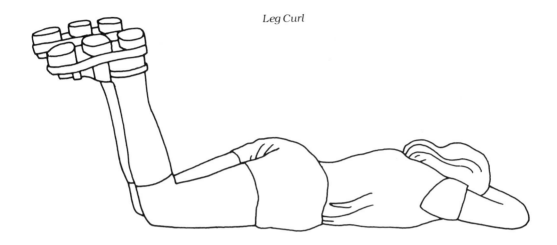

Leg Curl

sembles a hooded cobra half raising itself up from the ground.) It's a simple exercise. Lie face down on the floor, and put your hands behind your head, interlacing your fingers. Spread your feet apart a little for support. Now raise your chest off the floor as high as you can and hold that position for 5 or 10 seconds, whichever is possible. Now lower yourself back down. Do this five times at first, then as you get stronger increase repetitions to ten. Also to increase the intensity of the exercise, gradually increase the length of time you hold your chest up to 30 seconds each time.

Hamstring muscles. It's possible to strengthen your hamstring muscles when you're not on your bike, but for this you will need special resistance equipment. The exercise, called leg curls, requires that you either get a pair of weight shoes, or boots, which are basically heavy metal sandals with slots in them for adding weight, or some type of resistance equipment that you can use to exercise your legs in the position shown. If you use weight boots, all you have to do after strapping them on is lie on your stomach with your legs straight out on the floor and close together. Slowly lift your legs as high as possible and then lower them to the floor just as slowly. Start with five and work up to ten repetitions. Increase the weight as you feel your leg strength increasing.

Quadriceps. A problem that often plagues cyclists is called biker's knee. It's a painful knee condition that often comes when you have strained the ligament around your kneecap. There are various ways to alleviate this problem. If your knee hurts as you pedal, one of the simpler suggestions doctors offer is to use a lower gear, which will put less strain on that joint. The strain on your knee may have been the result of making it work too hard, pushing pedals in too high a gear.

Another possible cause of biker's knee pain is improper position of the feet on the pedals. If your toes point in too far or out too far, you can strain your knee ligaments unevenly, and pain is the result. If that seems to be your problem, an expensive but practical solution is to buy a pair of bicycling shoes with cleats on the bottom. These will hold your feet in a fixed position on the pedals and keep them from shifting one way or the other.

A final solution recommended by doctors is to strengthen the muscles, called quadriceps, around the knee. There is a simple exercise called the *Leg Lift,* which you can do with a pair of weight boots or even a small bucket. Sit on the edge of a table and put on a pair of 5-pound (2-kilograms) weight boots. A less-expensive alternative is to get an old paint can, fill it with sand until it weighs 5 pounds (2 kilograms), and hang it from your foot as shown in the illustration. To exercise, slowly raise your weighted foot until your leg is almost fully extended. Then slowly lower it back down. Do this five to ten times for each leg set, and do four sets of each. If you plan to increase weight, do it in small increments, no more than 2 pounds (1 kilogram).

Training with rollers

Opinions are divided in the cycling world over the benefits of using rollers. All serious riders use them; it is just a matter of how much and how often. In winter, when the weather is bad, rollers enable you to maintain a regular mileage. But rollers are no substitute for actually getting out on the road. For one thing, they will not teach you bike handling techniques, and worse still, if they are used for a prolonged period of time in an enclosed room or space (especially if it is heated) they will not be as beneficial aerobically as riding outdoors.

If you plan to take up cycling seriously, however, sooner or later you will need a set of rollers. Before a long race they are a very good way of warming-up quickly and at track events they are a basic part of in-field equipment.

Leg Lift

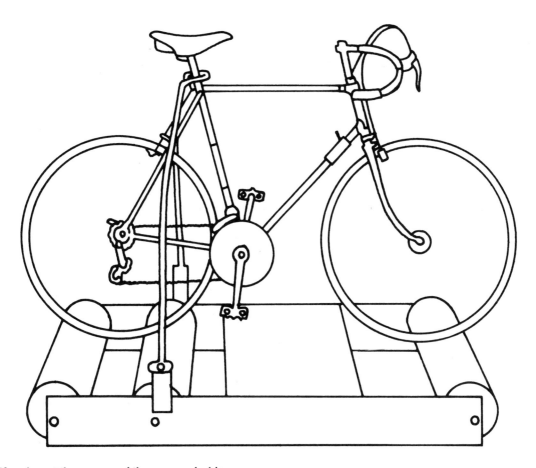

*If you've got the space and the unquenchable
urge to ride even when the weather is off,
bicycle rollers are the way for you to go.*

Chapter 3

RIDING TECHNIQUES

Have you ever noticed how natural most children look on their bicycles? Their motions are loose, supple, and relaxed. That's the way adults should ride also. But adults, ironically enough, often must learn what children can do instinctively. However, keeping in mind that there's no one way to ride a bike, here are some tips and techniques to help you feel comfortable and relaxed on your bicycle.

SETTING UP THE BIKE

We're assuming, of course, that you have a bicycle that's the proper size for your body (see Chapter 1). But even if the frame fits you, there's still the matter of saddle adjustment.

Height

Most people set their saddles much too low, so they can't properly extend their legs for maximum power. When the pedal is at the bottom of its stroke, your leg should be almost fully extended. The difficulty comes in defining "almost." Here's a good rule of

thumb: Get a friend to support the bicycle while you sit on the saddle in the normal riding position. Move the pedal to the bottom of its stroke (this is not the 6 o'clock position, where the pedal is closest to the ground, but at approximately the 7 o'clock position, where the pedal crank is aligned with the seat tube). Wearing the shoes you plan to bicycle in, place your heel flat on the pedal. Can you fully extend your leg and lock your knee? Fine. Your seat position is perfect. Now, when you pedal normally, with the ball of your foot on the pedal, your leg will be slightly and properly bent.

If you cannot lock your knee with your heel on the pedal without pushing yourself off the saddle, of course you'll have to raise the seat. If you find you've been riding your bike with the saddle much too low, requiring an upward adjustment of, say, 1 inch (2½ centimeters) or more, you may find yourself frightened about raising it that much. Raise the saddle ¼ inch

The proper saddle height can be gauged by leg extension, as shown in the illustration right. It's worth your trouble to do this carefully, or else you'll end up both riding uncomfortably and nursing sore legs and lower back pains.

(½ centimeter) at a time over a 4-week period, or thereabouts, until you get to the perfect height.

Some cyclists like to find the perfect saddle height more scientifically, and for them there's the Thomas Method, named after Vaughan Thomas, who published a study on the subject in 1967. Thomas, after testing over 100 bicycle racers, discovered that for maximum performance the distance from the saddle to the pedal should be 109 percent of the length of your leg measured from the crotch to the floor.

You can use the Thomas Method if you wish, but most cyclists don't. And while it might be a bit more scientific, the Thomas Method still produces basically the same result as the aforementioned heel method. It's also harder than you might think to get accurate inseam and pedal-to-saddle measurements if you don't have an experienced tailor and a bicycle-frame builder on hand.

Other Saddle Adjustments

Your saddle may also be moved forward, backward, and tilted on its clip. For most people, especially beginners, the saddle should be centered over the seat post. But after you find your cycling style, you may wish to experiment: Push the seat back a little if you find you prefer pedaling slowly but powerfully; move it slightly forward if you tend to pedal quickly but lightly. Remember: Should you adjust the saddle drastically forward or backward, it will affect the *reach*; that is, the proper distance from the seat to the handlebars. After resetting the saddle, once again use the forearm-stretch method (described in Chapter 1) to make sure your arms will be neither overextended nor cramped in

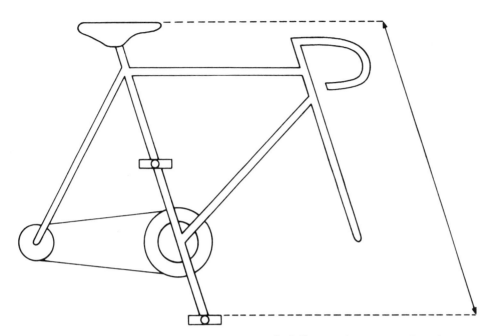

The Thomas Method for determining saddle height looks like fun if you enjoy calculus or playing with your calculator, but its results don't really differ from the simpler heel method illustrated on page 46. It is also dependent upon having exact measurements of your inseam and the maximum saddle-to-pedal extension.

reaching the handlebars. You may find you must buy a shorter or longer stem to accommodate your new saddle position. Then again, you may decide that the good old center position wasn't so bad after all, especially since it saves you the time and expense of taking apart your handlebars.

As for proper tilt, most cyclists prefer the nose of the saddle pointed slightly upward. But some also like their seat perfectly level. Having the saddle pointed downward is never a good idea because when it's in that position, you're liable to slip off your bicycle.

Handlebar Height

Whether you've got flat handlebars or the dropped racing kind, you're best off with the top of the stem at about the same height as the saddle or slightly lower.

RIDING THE BIKE

Now you're ready to ride. There are many things to learn. But the most important thing is to learn how to relax when you're riding.

Relaxing

There's a trick to this, and it's in your elbows. Keep them bent at all times. Every few minutes as you ride, look at your arms. Are they as stiff as high-tension cables? Elbows locked? Are your hands frozen in a death grip on the handlebars? If so, then you're not relaxed. Besides wearing out your body with muscular tension, this unrelaxed position actually endangers you.

So for a relaxed position, keep your elbows bent; the rest of your body should automatically loosen up as well. And a loose body acts as a giant shock absorber. For example, if you suddenly hit a pothole or any sort of hole or bump, your bent arms will help soak up the shock, and this could prevent you and your bike from toppling to the pavement. Keeping your elbows bent is especially important when cycling over rough pavement or crossing railroad tracks. And since any two-wheeled vehicle is steered primarily by shifting body weight, keeping your body relaxed allows you to steer more quickly and avoid obstructions of all kinds.

Besides the elbows, other key areas to watch are the shoulders, neck, and hands. Many cyclists hold tension in their shoulders, especially if their bikes have dropped handlebars. Don't hunch your shoulders. Hunching won't protect you from anything. And occasionally roll your head in a circular motion to loosen up neck muscles. Changing positions on the handlebars should help keep your hands and fingers relaxed.

Changing Gears

Although shifting gears is not the key to skillful riding, if you don't master the basics, shifting can become an obsession that will ruin bike-riding for you.

Shifting a 3-speed is no problem. Shift only when coasting. Stop pedaling, and then flip the lever, turn the twist grip, back-pedal, or do whatever it is that shifts the gears on your particular model.

Ten-speeds are tougher to master. First, you must be pedaling when you shift (never back-pedal while shifting, for that could ruin the entire gear mechanism).

A 10-speed has two shift levers: one on the left and one on the right. The one on the left side controls the chainwheel shifter up front. Pulling this lever down pushes the chain onto the outside, larger chainwheel and by doing so gives you a higher gear (harder

Poor Riding Position

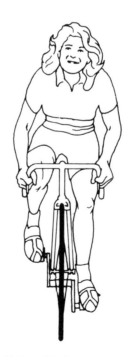

Relaxed Riding Position

Poor Riding Position

to pedal, but more speed). Pushing it up shifts the chain back to the inner, smaller chainwheel. (On Sun Tour brand front derailleurs, this procedure is reversed.)

Most of your shifting, however, will be done with the right-side lever, which controls the rear derailleur. Pulling the right lever down shifts the chain from the smaller (higher) gears to the larger (lower) gears. There are, of course, five gears on the back wheel. But you will not find five clearly marked gear positions on your right gear shift. There are no stops or set positions like on a car (the one exception is the Shimano Positron derailleur, which does have five click-stops). What this means is that you must feel—and hear—when the chain has properly seated itself on the gear you want. With experience, this becomes easy. But it will take a little time to gain this experience.

For example, when starting out, you may shift two or three gears at once by mistake. You may also shift past the sprocket you want by half a gear. This means the chain will be hung up between gears, where it will bounce around, making a racket and losing most of your cycling energy to excess friction. When you hear that chattering sound, fiddle with your gear lever back and forth until the chain seats properly.

The key to crisp, smooth shifting is a brisk, light, even pedaling rhythm. Derailleurs are most often damaged on steep hill climbs when a rider is hacking the pedals up and down with powerful but awkward strokes. Hill climbs are especially tough because you're shifting into lower gears, which on the rear wheel are the larger sprockets. It's harder to move the chain from a small sprocket to a large sprocket, anyway, and shifting into

them under strain is known as *jamming.* To avoid jamming, shift into low gears before the going gets really difficult. As you approach a hill, shift down immediately, before you start huffing and puffing and your legs get heavy and slow.

A final piece of advice: Don't be so concerned about being in the right gear that you spend more time looking at your derailleur than you do looking at the road. It happens. Experienced cyclists have ridden directly into cars or off the roads because they were looking at their rear derailleurs. With practice, you will not have to look, you will be able to feel which gear you are in.

Cadence. Now that you know how to shift gears, which do you use, and when? This is a time-honored cycling question. Of course, you'll have to use low gears for going up hills, and big gears for racing down the other side. But for general terrain, do you stick to relatively low gears and pedal very fast, or use high gears and pedal slowly? Find a group of cyclists and pose this question to them, and you'll be in a heated argument for hours. There are three terms you should know: cadence, twiddling, and plunging. As explained in Chapter 2, cadence is the number of times you rotate the pedals every minute over a consistent period of time. A *twiddler* is a cyclist with a fast cadence, say 90 revolutions per minute (rpm). To maintain this foot speed, the cyclist uses lower gears. A *plunger* pushes high gears at a slower cadence, say 60 rpm.

Unless you're going to be a sprint racer, twiddling seems to make the most sense. A high cadence and endurance seem to go hand in hand, and endurance is more important to touring cyclists than great bursts of speed. Most inexperienced bikers pedal too slowly in too high a gear. So it might pay to count the number of pedal revolutions you average over a 5- or 10-minute ride. If it's over 50 rpm, you're unusually fast for a beginner. But 50 rpm is still on the slow side. We'd recommend dropping down into lower gears and trying to average somewhere between 60 and 90 rpm.

However, don't get carried away worrying about cadence. Whether you're a twiddler or a plunger depends a lot on your body type, your metabolism, and even your personality. If you're a muscular type who feels comfortable pushing big gears at 60 rpm while your friends twiddle alongside you at 90 rpm, there's no reason to change if you cycle the distance you want to go.

In general, plunging tests the strength of your legs; twiddling tests the condition of your lungs, heart, and cardiovascular system. If your legs begin to hurt, shift to a lower gear and increase your cadence. If your breathing becomes difficult and your heart starts to pound, shift up and pedal slower. That's all there is to it.

Toe clips and straps keep the ball of your foot properly positioned on the pedal, which gives you more thrust and avoids injury to your arches because it stops you from using them to pedal with.

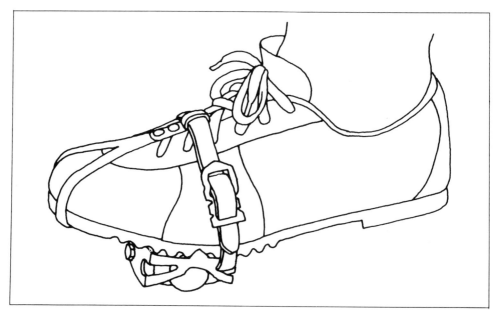

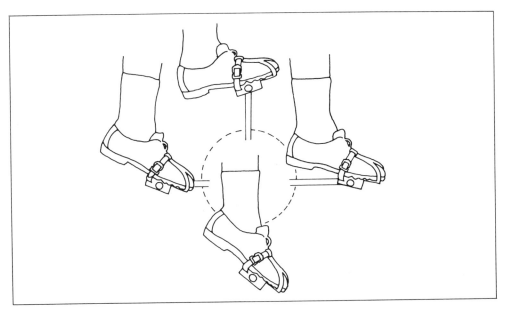

*Ankling is a pedaling technique that requires
you to hold your foot in these four positions so
that your body is relatively stable while riding
and your legs and feet do the work.*

Classic cycling techniques requires you to find your cadence and then maintain it at all costs. This means that if you discover 78 rpm is best for you, you must always pedal at 78 rpm—on the flats, uphill or down. This can be done, but it requires a ridiculous amount of gear shifting. Many champion road racers don't adhere to such strict principles, and neither need you.

Pedaling Correctly

Don't waste energy. Many cyclists roll side-to-side and rock back-and-forth on the saddle to get more power into their pedal strokes. It doesn't work. All that motion is wasted energy. Keep your body relatively motionless from the waist up; the upper body should be anchored (in a relaxed way, of course) to offset the powerful strokes of your legs.

Much is made of proper pedaling methods. But all you really have to remember is to pedal with the ball of your foot—and not your arch—on the pedal. If you have toe clips and straps on your pedals, they will hold your foot in the proper position.

A pedaling technique that racers are taught to use is called *pulling up*. Most of us push down one foot, then give it a free ride on the upswing while we push down the other one. A racer will keep the straps tight and pull up with one foot while pushing down with the other. This technique obviously improves your power, but it's tiring!

There's also a pedaling technique known as *ankling*. This requires you to hold your foot in four different positions, as shown in the illustration above, as it makes each revolution. Despite the fact that it has got incredible publicity in recent years, we don't think that ankling is of much importance. High-speed motion pictures of professionals' feet show that none of them use this technique.

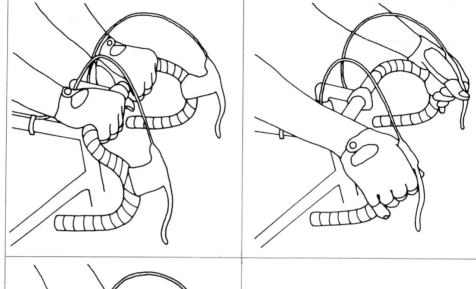

Dropped handlebars enable the rider to use a variety of hand positions.

Hand Positions

The nice thing about dropped handlebars is the variety of hand positions they allow you. The illustrations on this page are three basic positions, but there are numerous variations of these. You're bound to find a favorite position, and that's fine. But do shift your hands around, especially on long rides. Your hands can get numb very quickly—and sometimes without your realizing it—especially in chilly weather. Then when you have to hit the brakes in a hurry, you find you're cramped up.

Steering and Stopping

Obviously, the ability to keep your bike traveling in a straight line can be crucial, especially in heavy traffic. Practice by following the painted lines in parking lots. The best way to keep your bicycle going straight is not by staring at the road in front of your wheel. Look straight ahead at a point about 30 to 40 feet (9.1 to 12.2 meters) down the road instead. Also keep in mind that every time you look behind over your shoulder to check on following traffic, your bike will tend to swing out into the road a few feet. So make sure no one is alongside when you attempt these rearview glances.

When taking a sharp corner, we recommend you coast through it rather than pedal. Always keep your inside pedal up at the 12 o'clock position; otherwise it could hit the pavement as you lean inward and send you sprawling. Don't attempt to shift gears while cornering. And brake the bike to a safe speed before entering the curve. If you must brake on a corner, only use the brake on the rear wheel.

As for braking in general, many cyclists forget they have two brakes: a front and a rear. The rear-brake lever is normally located on the right side of the handlebars, and since most people are righthanded they tend to rely only on this brake. But use both. While riding, most of your weight is on the rear wheel, so rear braking gives the better traction. But when you make a hard emergency stop, your weight will shift forward, in which case the front brake becomes more effective. So learn to use both brakes together for the strongest, safest stops.

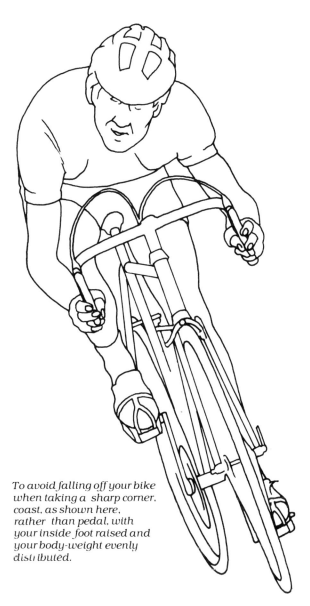

To avoid falling off your bike when taking a sharp corner, coast, as shown here, rather than pedal, with your inside foot raised and your body-weight evenly distributed.

Chapter 4

BICYCLE TOURING

There are faster ways to travel than hopping on a bicycle and pedaling from here to there. And there are certainly less strenuous ways. But it's hard to think of a method of transportation that is as much fun and as interesting as bicycling.

Most travel today is a sterile experience in which you sit sealed inside a car, train, or plane and blur past the surrounding scenery without ever feeling any connection with it. This is some people's idea of the way traveling ought to be, without any strain.

If you feel differently, maybe now is the time to load up your bicycle and take a trip. Bicycle touring is the most rewarding way to see the world: it's healthy; it's fun; and it's certainly an inexpensive way to go. There is never an energy crisis for the bicycle tourist.

THE TOURING BIKE

If you have the time, the patience, and the stamina, you can travel just about any distance you want on almost any kind of bike. One spunky Irish nurse named Dervla Murphy traveled from India to Ireland on a very unsleek 36-pound (16-kilogram) bicycle with only three gears.

10-Speed

As a general rule, you can travel very comfortably with what is now the standard model for touring: the 10-speed bike. This is not to say you couldn't get by with a 5-speed bike, a 15-speed, or one of the newer Japanese 12-speed bikes. You can. It's just that the 10-speed is a good compromise. It offers you a broader gearing range than the 5-speed, and because it's a little less complicated than the 12- or 15-speed, it's less likely to give you trouble.

The one aspect of your 10-speed you should be most concerned about is gearing. Since you will be pedaling with more weight and will have to work a little harder going up hills, you should be especially careful about having the right low gears to help you

The 10-speed bike has become the standard touring vehicle used by most bikers for these reasons: it is relatively lightweight, can be *relatively inexpensive, and its range of gears allows the biker to take on most types of terrain without reaching utter exhaustion.*

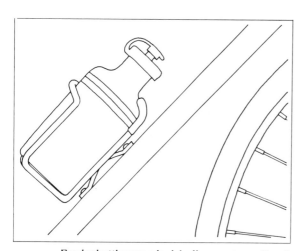

Feeder bottles may look bulky, unstreamlined, and unglamourous, but looks don't mean everything when you've been traveling some distance—you'll be thankful to have that feeder bottle from which you can take small sips of water.

do this. Ordinarily, the high gears you get with a standard 10-speed bike are fine for touring, but this is not always true for the low end of the range.

Gearing is measured in inches by a complex formula. For deciding if your bike has low enough gearing, all you have to remember is that your lowest gear should at least be under 40 inches and as close to 20 or 25 inches as you can get.

Accessories

Some accessories you might be tempted to buy are usually not worth getting. Odometers or speedometers, generator lights, and big rearview mirrors are not usually worth the investment. The following sections discuss some accessories that are essentials.

Feeders, Pumps, and Toe Clips. You'll probably want to get a feeder, or water bottle, and a frame for it to attach to your bike. Of course, you'll also need a good bicycle pump and if your pedals don't already have them, toe clips.

Reflectors and Carrying Racks. For safety's sake, you should have a red rear reflector. This is usually attached to another accessory worth buying, the carrying rack, a metal frame that fits over your back wheel and to which you attach your bike panniers or saddlebags. The best kind are solid rigid frameworks that won't bend or sway under the load of the bike bags.

Lights. Unfortunately, there isn't a bike light made that does a really good job of lighting the road ahead. At night, you should make sure you can be seen. One gadget that is helpful is the French armband light. It is essentially a T-shaped, two-faced flashlight with a white plastic lens in front and a red plastic lens in the back. It is equipped with a small band or belt you use to attach to your leg (not to your arm, as the name suggests) just below your knee, usually on your left leg. As you pedal along, the light bobs up and down with your leg, making you much more noticeable to a driver coming up behind you in the night.

The best type of light is the kind that can easily be detached from the bike. One particular brand suited to bicycling and camping is the Wonder Light. Sold both in Europe and the United States and made in France, the light has a holder that clamps to your handlebars and which also allows you to take the light off the bike when you need it by simply slipping it out of the holder.

Locks. If you are traveling through cities you will need some type of bike security. The more expensive and better-equipped your bike is, the more tempting a target it will be for a potential thief. To discourage this kind of

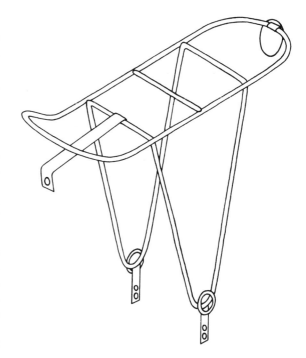

Carrying racks are handy both for long distance tours and for running local errands. They should be solid and rigid.

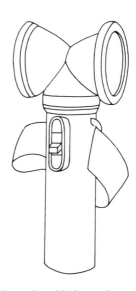

The French armband light can be useful if you simply must ride at night—at least other people will be able to spot you from back and front. But be aware that some places have strict regulations about the kind of lights you should use if you night-ride.

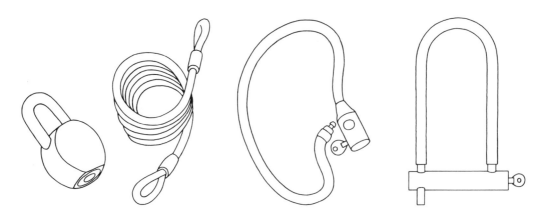

A case-hardened chain or cable with a sturdy, separate padlock (left) or a one-unit cablelock (center) are good buys. The U-shaped lock (right) is your best bet if you live in any American metropolitan area—they are virtually impossible to break through.

interest, you can probably get by with a lightweight cable and small lock to attach the bike to a signpost or tree.

Fenders. One bicycle item that some feel is optional but you may wish you had on a rainy day is a pair of fenders, or mudguards. Ten-speed bikes are seldom sold with a pair and there is a kind of snob appeal about riding a bike without them, probably because it gives you a bike-racer look. Unfortunately, if you're riding along on wet roads, this means that there is nothing to stop the water from splashing up into your face and up your back. To avoid this kind of discomfort, you don't have to go out and buy a set of full-length heavy metal fenders. Most bike shops now sell short lightweight plastic fenders that keep most water from splashing up and over you.

PREPARING YOUR ROUTE

Planning and taking a bike trip is not the difficult challenge it sometimes seems to many people. If you know how to ride a bike and know how to make minor adjustments and repairs, such as changing a flat tire, you can travel on your bike.

How far you go will depend on your stamina, as well as how much time and money you have. If you cannot visualize yourself sitting on a bike, pedaling hours and hours all day long, and maybe are worried about how you'll like it, take a short bike trip.

Pick a spot about 15 to 20 miles (25 to 33 kilometers) from your home. Listen to the weather forecasts, and on a day when you reasonably expect to have decent weather, schedule a round trip. Take along everything mentioned in the tool kit list (page 61), and take your time. The idea is to spend a day on the bicycle to see how it feels. Take your time, enjoy the scenery, notice the smooth steady rhythm of pedaling you settle into as you ride. Could you see yourself traveling like this for a weekend? For a week? For 2 weeks? If the answer to any of these questions is yes, then you're certainly ready to ride.

Using a Map

The first step in planning any bicycle trip is know your route. To do that, you need a map and the special mindset or mentality of the two-wheeled traveler. Your days riding will be measured in time as well as mileage or kilometers. Depending on different variables, you should figure that your average day's riding would cover between 25 and 40 miles (42 to 64 kilometers) and take about 4 to 5 hours. The beginning rider should plan small, about 25 miles (42 kilometers) riding time a day.

Traffic. As you read a map, focus on two things: traffic and terrain, the potential enemies of bicyclists. Whenever possible, always plot your route along a secondary road. The best routes are those that parallel main roads, which will drain most of the cars from the routes you'll want to take. Many drivers are in too much of a hurry to slow down and enjoy the scenery on these slower roads and, except for local traffic, they become almost the exclusive domain of the bicyclist.

Terrain. Even if land contours aren't marked on your map, you can still tell what kind of terrain you'll have to ride over on your trip. As you read your map, look for clues such as streams and rivers. They are found in valleys where the land is flat, so if your road runs alongside the stream, the odds are that it too is probably flat. If the road crosses the stream or if the stream itself has a snaky, twisting and turning look, and the road runs alongside it, be on the alert for hills and hard pedaling. On days that include this part of the route, you might want to schedule a little less distance than you do usually.

PREPARING YOUR BICYCLE

Once you think you have plotted a good route and have it marked out on your map, you are almost ready to start out. Before you go anywhere, though, always make it a habit to give your bicycle a pretrip inspection the day before the trip at the latest so that you have time to correct any problems and buy new parts you might need. Also make it a habit to give your bike a quick inspection every morning while you are getting ready to start out on the road. The check list is short and simple.

Tires
Inspect the tires carefully for cuts, bruises, and pieces of glass or even sharp pebbles imbedded in the tread. Make sure they are inflated to the recommended pressure (usually stamped on the side-wall), and if they look a little too worn or cut up, don't hesitate to replace them. The newer your tires, the fewer problems you're likely to have.

Brakes
Check the brake pads. If they look too worn, replace them. They are inexpensive to buy and can make a real difference in riding safely. Also, grab both brake levers and squeeze hard! If the levers come within an inch (2½ centimeters) or less of the handlebars, they need to be tightened. (Chapter 7 on bike maintenance will tell you how.) Inspect your cables both for the brakes and derailleurs at the connection points. Brake cables that are too frazzled and frayed looking should also be replaced.

Saddle
How your seat is adjusted can make the difference between a pleasant bike ride and a day or more of torture on your two wheels. The important adjustment is the height of the saddle. It should be up high enough so that when your foot reaches the low point of a pedal stroke your leg should be fully extended with your foot resting flat on the pedal. If the saddle is higher or lower than this, your pedaling will put undue strain on your legs and knees. For other saddle adjustments, see Chapter 3.

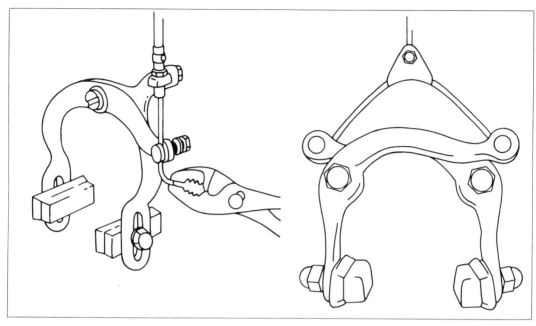

Brake cables and brake pads on both side-pull brakes (left) and center-pull brakes (right) should be inspected and replaced or adjusted fairly frequently.

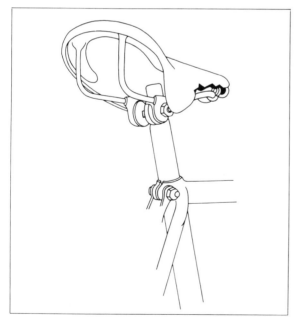

How to adjust the angle of your saddle is a choice best left to experimentation and personal taste. The height of the saddle is the only more-or-less fixed measurement and should, of course, depend on your leg length.

Pedals and Chain, Nuts and Bolts

Spin your pedals. They should spin freely and easily. If not, put a drop of oil in the side where they are attached to the cranks. Back-pedal your chain, and listen closely. Hear anything? If you hear a gritty scraping noise, there is probably dirt and dust deposited around the pivot points of your chain link. Wipe off the chain with an old towel, and using a screwdriver, flick out any obvious flecks of debris you can spot between the links. A cleaner chain will mean easier pedaling. Finally, check for loose nuts and bolts, especially on your wheels (if you don't have quick-release hubs) and where your rear carrier rack (you should have one) is attached to the bicycle frame. Do a quick once over with a wrench and screwdriver. Some of these bolts and nuts may shake loose after a rough ride.

Basic Tool Kit

One last thing of concern is a tool kit. If you are traveling for 2 days or 20 days, at the very least you'll need the following items:

• A bicycle pump (with the appropriate Presta or Schraeder valve connection for your tires)

• A tube repair kit if you have clincher tires or a spare sew-up tire if you have sew-ups and rim tape or glue

• A set of three tire irons if your bike has clincher tires

• A 6-inch (15-centimeter) long adjustable crescent wrench (the best you can afford)

• A tire pressure gauge. Make sure you have the appropriate kind for your tires. Clincher tires need Schraeder valve gauges, while sew-up tires take Presta valve gauges.

Optional items for short (day) trips but an absolute necessity for long trips are the following:

• Two brand new tubes for clincher tires (or two new sew-up tires)

• A screwdriver with a ¼-inch (½-centimeter) blade

• A pair of pliers/wirecutters

• A handlebar bag or saddlebag to carry all this in

• A feeder bottle and cage, or carrier (or you could carry a large canteen for hot days)

• A well-read and well-marked map to help you on your way

PREPARE YOURSELF

Now that you've prepared your bike and marked your route, there are still a few final preparations to be made. Many people tend to worry too much about equipment. In fact they become obsessed with just the right color handlebar tape or the ideal feeder bottle, but more often than not, they lose their common sense when it comes to outfitting themselves.

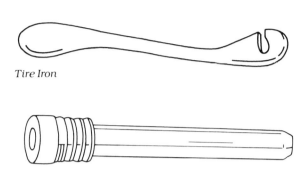

Tire Iron

Air Gauge

Helmets

The only piece of personal bicycle gear you should really worry about getting is a good bicycle helmet. Just about everything else is optional. One Canadian study of bicycle injuries found that when bones were broken, the first most common break was a collarbone. The second was a skull fracture.

While you could probably survive a broken collarbone without any serious after effects, you may not with a skull fracture. For that reason, worry about head protection first and about getting other personal equipment later. Fortunately there are a number of hard-shell helmets you can buy made exclusively for the bicyclist or

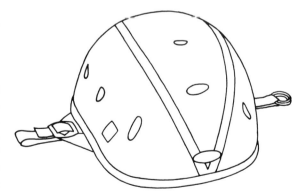

The hard-shell type of bicycle helmet offers the best protection against injuries like skull fracture and good ventilation.

just as good are the kind that kayakers and mountain climbers sometimes wear. The one rule of thumb in buying a touring helmet is not to get the so-called hairnet type of helmet, the type you sometimes see professional racers wear. This offers you practically no significant protection and is not worth the money.

Gloves

You might want to invest in a pair of bicycle gloves. These are special fingerless gloves with open-mesh backs and padded palms. Although your hand positions will change as you ride, most of the time you will be leaning a good part of your body weight on your hands, especially on the heel of each hand. During a long day of riding, your palms may get sore and tender from the jiggling of the road and the pressure of your weight. Gloves will help relieve that problem.

Shorts

Strictly optional are close-fitting cycling shorts. Usually equipped with an inner lining of soft chamois to protect your bottom, these minimize some of the abrasive action that comes with sitting on the slim saddle and moving your legs continually. These shorts are comfortable but also tend to be expensive. You can probably get by just as well with a comfortable pair of cotton shorts that have no heavy crotch seam, which will probably tend to rub or chafe your legs.

Jerseys

Although bicycle jerseys are attractive and give you a certain amount of flair, they are hardly necessary. It's not that they're not handy—they are equipped with several pockets big enough to hold a small lunch and a spare tire— it's just that unless you want to spend the money for these expensive articles of clothing, they are not absolutely essential to comfortable riding. A plain

cotton T-shirt, or sweatshirt in cooler weather, will work fine.

Shoes

The same holds true for those fancy bicycle shoes you may have seen people wear. If you plan to start bicycle racing, they may be worth buying, but the average bicycle tourist can get by very well with a pair of stiff-soled sneakers (plimsolls) or jogging shoes.

Rain Gear

One last item of clothing that you may want to include in your traveling kit is rain gear. Probably the most practical arrangement is a rain cape—basically a short bell-shaped waterproof poncho —along with a pair of rain chaps, or waterproof leggings for especially messy weather. Most of the time you probably won't even need the rain chaps. In fact, if the weather is warm and you're wearing shorts, the rain chaps would probably be too hot anyway. Rain suits—waterproof pants and jackets—generally aren't worth getting because they act like a sauna, trapping body heat and perspiration inside and getting you just as wet as if you had no protection at all. An inexpensive alternative to the rain cape and rain chaps is buying a cheap plastic poncho. This works almost as well, and if you are careful to tuck the back flap under your seat when you ride to keep it from flapping around, it will keep you reasonably dry and still allow for ventilation.

Bike Luggage

First, here are some general guidelines. Never carry anything on your body if you plan to bicycle a long distance. The reasons are very basic. Wearing a small knapsack or even backpack, as some people do when they bicycle, is an uncomfortable and dangerous way to travel. For one thing, the weight on your back simply puts more pressure on your bottom and hands as you ride. Over the span of several hours this takes its toll on your stamina. Also, the pack raises your center of gravity, making you and the bike less stable. In general, use your bike to carry the weight and your body to move your wheels along.

For most touring, a handlebar bag that attaches to the front of your bike and a pair of rear panniers that attach to your rear bicycle carrier are usually sufficient.

The piece of bike luggage that is probably most versatile is the handlebar bag. There are a variety of models and styles, most of which are well-made and practical. Some attach directly to your handlebars, while others attach to a separate rack you attach to your handlebars. Whatever style you choose, there are certain features you should look for.

First, the bag should not interfere with your hand brakes in any way. It should give you plenty of room to grab and squeeze the brake levers and should not crimp or press down on the brake cables. It should also ride high enough off the handlebars so that it doesn't droop down and drag on your front wheel.

Another feature to look for is the material. Bags made of water-resistant nylon are just about as sturdy as canvas and a little lighter. Also look for handlebar bags that you can open and get into easily as you are riding. In general, the flap should open away from you. Another handy feature many bags have is a clear-plastic map holder that is usually attached to the outside of the bag. It will let you read the map and keep it dry and clean at the same time. Since you'll probably be keeping valuables as well as handy items in your handlebar bag, it should also be easily detachable from the bike so that you can take it with you when you

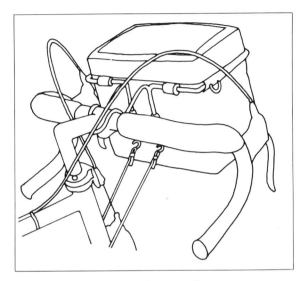

A handlebar bag is the only piece of luggage you'll need for a day-long run. They come in all sizes and prices, but make sure that the type you select doesn't interfere with your hand brakes.

park. Some bags have carrying or shoulder straps, another desirable feature.

Even the lowest-priced panniers are quite expensive, so you should shop around before you buy. The bags should attach and detach from your rear carrier easily. Those that attach to the carrier with straps tend to slip and work loose as you ride. Better models use some type of elastic or spring and hook attachment, which gives a little with road bounces and still holds firm. A second feature is that the panniers should ride far enough back so they don't interfere with the heel of your foot as you pedal, and don't interfere with the functioning of your rear derailleur.

Like the handlbar bag, the better panniers are made of heavy-duty nylon coated for waterproofing and usually have some sort of stiffening in the back of them so that they don't sag into your spokes or press on the derailleur. If you can, also try to get a

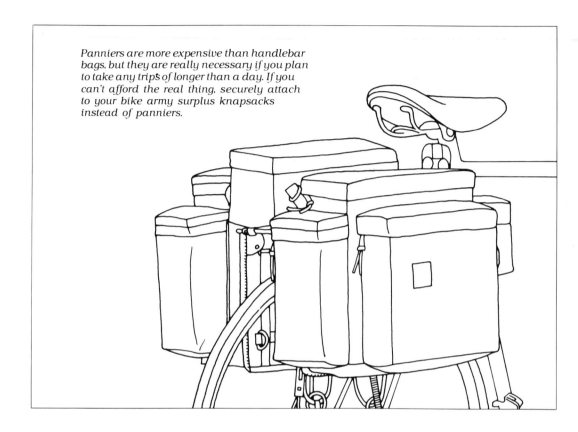

Panniers are more expensive than handlebar bags, but they are really necessary if you plan to take any trips of longer than a day. If you can't afford the real thing, securely attach to your bike army surplus knapsacks instead of panniers.

pair of panniers with at least one small outside pocket where you can keep items you want to get to in a hurry, such as a first aid kit, spare tires or tubes, a rain poncho, or anything else lightweight that you might have to get to in a minor emergency.

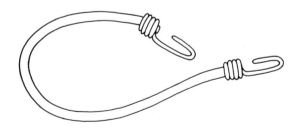

Sandows, or bungee cords, come in a variety of lengths and are much more convenient than using ropes or any other method of strapping down luggage.

As with the handlebar bags, don't assume that bigger is always better. Buying bags that are too large for your needs might tempt you to pack more than you'll ever use. Since you are the one who will have to provide the power to haul all your equipment, make it easy on yourself. Pack your bags as light as you can.

Sandows. The only other accessories you should worry about for touring are heavy elastic ropes called sandows, or sometimes bungee cords. They come equipped with a large hook at each end. They're available in various lengths from 2 to 6 feet (½ to 2 meters). If you get two 2- or 3-foot (½- or 1-meter) sandows, you should be able to strap down just about everything to your rear carrier. They're an absolute necessity for every bike tourist.

Packing

Two factors will determine just what you should take on your trip: how long you'll be traveling and in what style, as a noncamper or as a camper.

First, some general guidelines about packing. Weight should be your main concern—how much and how you pack it on your bike. Try to keep the maximum total weight of what you carry in your bags and on your rear carrier below about 30 pounds (roughly 15 kilograms). As you pack, follow this rule: When in doubt, leave it out. The more experience you have traveling, then, of course, the better you'll get at packing.

Loading the Panniers. The most critical part of packing is loading your panniers. Each should have equivalent amounts of weight to keep the load balanced. They don't have to be equal down to the last gram, but come as close as you can. Use a bathroom scale to weigh them if you're in doubt. As you pack the panniers, make sure to concentrate the heavier items low and to the inside of the bags. This will give you a lower and more stable center of gravity.

Packing List for Noncampers. Below is a suggested packing list for non-camping bike tourists, those who plan to stay in hostels, bed and breakfasts, hotels or motels as they travel. This will serve you for a weekend trip or a week-long trip.

In the handlebar bag, pack these items:
- A tool kit (see the list, page 61)
- Two new spare tires for sew-ups or spare tubes for clincher tires
- A map
- A pair of sunglasses (to protect your eyes from sun glare, random insects, and gravel thrown up by passing cars)
- A hat (to shield your head on hot, sunny days)
- A tube repair kit (if you have clincher tires)
- A first aid kit (band-aids, or plasters; gauze, bandage tape; antiseptic cream or ointment; aspirin; tweezers). This is a must.
- A Swiss army type knife equipped with at least a knife blade, corkscrew, screwdriver, can opener, and bottle opener
- A pair of bicycling gloves

Optional:
- A camera and film and film mailers
- A notebook and pen
- A guidebook

In the panniers, put these items:
- A bag of toilet articles (soap, toothpaste, toothbrush, shampoo, comb, and shaving gear)
- A towel (a dark color preferably; it doesn't show the dirt)
- Two pairs of cotton or wool socks
- A sewing kit
- Two changes of underwear
- A pair of long pants or a skirt
- A sweater or down vest
- Two dark cotton T-shirts
- A long-sleeved shirt or blouse
- A lightweight nylon jacket or windshirt to keep off the morning chill

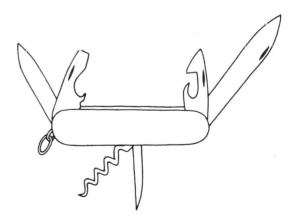

Anybody who has ever been on a trip with a Swiss army type knife will be able to attest to its incredible usefulness.

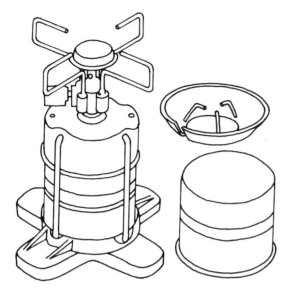

Touring from campground to campground means cooking for yourself: and now, thanks to the growing popularity of backpacking, there are two types of compact and dependable stoves available: one uses liquid gas or kerosene, the other uses butane gas.

• A rain poncho or rain cape (rain chaps are optional)
• A flashlight and extra batteries
The following items are optional but helpful:
• Six plastic bags to put your clothes in. Even the best panniers aren't totally waterproof.
• A rear brake cable (It can be cut shorter to fit the front brakes as well.)
• A rear derailleur cable (It can also be trimmed short for the front.)
• A roll of nylon fiber or electrician's tape (will come in handy for dozens of quick repairs)
On your bike you should have the following items:
• A feeder bottle and cage, or carrier
• A rear carrier rack
• A bicycle pump and holder
• A red rear reflector
• Two or three sandows, or bungee cords

And on your head, of course, you should have a bicycle helmet.
Packing List for Campers. The more weight you carry, the more practice you should have riding with it. This is particularly true if you plan to take a bike trip that will take you from campground to campground. In addition to everything listed for noncampers, you will also be carrying:
• A sleeping bag with stuff sack
• A sleeping pad or mattress
• A tent
• A small rubber mallet for pounding in tent pegs
• A compact stove
• A set of silverware (knife, fork, spoon)
• A compact mess kit (cup, frying pan, plate, and small pot)

If you plan to go camping, try to arrange to share the load with someone else. One person carrying the tent **and** stove, for example, and the other **carrying** two sleeping bags and the mess kit.

If you can afford it, the best—that is lightest and warmest—sleeping bag is one filled with 2 pounds (1 kilogram) of down for late spring and summer camping. Slightly less expensive, but almost as efficient, is the type filled with synthetic insulation, which is a little heavier but, unlike down, dries more quickly when it has been wet.

When it comes to tents, for comfort's sake, try to get one that is designed for one more person than the total who will occupy it. If two people will be using it, get a three-person model; if three, buy a four-person tent. The reason is that your gear tends to occupy the space of one more person. Nylon is the lightest tent material, and the most efficient design is the kind that has a separate fly, or waterproof roof. With this design, the inner part, the nonwaterproof roof, breathes, that is

Your mess kit should be lightweight and compact—in a word, aluminum. The typical mess kit usually includes a pot with lid, a cup, a frying pan, and a plate.

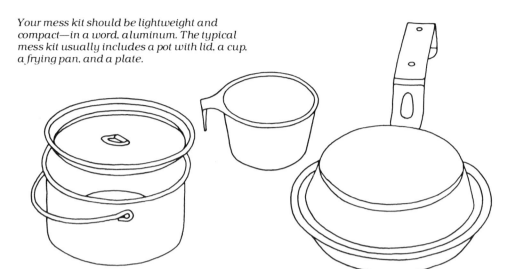

releases the moisture that can collect in a tent and still be shielded from rain and hot sun by the second roof.

For sleeping, the best compromise is a foam sleeping pad, which is lighter than an air mattress, will never go flat from a puncture, and is almost as comfortable.

And as for your cooking gear, practically any camping store or army sur- plus store will have inexpensive aluminum cooksets and ingenious knife, fork, and spoon sets. For your cooking, an excellent choice is the French-made Bleuet stove, a compact camping stove that uses a disposable cartridge of butane gas. Refills are widely available in camping supply stores both in the United States and in Europe.

Chapter 5

TAKING A TOUR

In the past 10 years, the surge of people traveling by bicycle has generated many kinds of travel services designed to simplify the trip and turn it into an enjoyable adventure. Today the traveling cyclist is no longer looked on as a weird creature of the road, but is considered to be part of a new breed of tourist who gets around with flair.

TRANSPORTING YOUR BIKE

Very often, you have to use public transportation to get you and your bike to the starting point of your journey. This can get very complicated, but you will save yourself a lot of travel headaches if, well in advance of your trip, you call or write the specific transportation company you plan to use to find out their policy on transporting bicycles.

This holds true even if you've shipped your bike by plane, train, or bus with the same company before. Never assume, for example, that one airline's rule for shipping your bike this year will be the same as it was last year. Maybe last year you were able to just roll your bike up to the ticket counter and check it in. This year that same airline might not consider transporting your bike unless it's completely broken down and packed in a cardboard carton.

Always attach some kind of identification to your bike, such as a luggage tag with your name and address on it, to your rear carrying rack or the underside of your saddle. As an added precaution, write out your name and address on a card or piece of paper and slip it down the seat tube. That way if someone else claims your bike, you can always fish out this paper as final proof. Finally, if you own a foreign-made bike and will be traveling out of the country, make sure to take along a bill of sale or some proof of payment. This especially applies if your bike is new and you also plan to be traveling to the country where the bike was made. Suppose, for example, you own a Peugeot bike and plan a trip to France. When you return to your own country, it might be difficult convincing the Customs Officer that you didn't buy the bike in France unless you have proof of payment. Some national customs offices, such as those in the United States, will let you register your foreign-made goods before you leave the country to avoid the problem of customs duty. Their registry slip can substitute for the bill of sale.

THE FLYING BIKE

As we mentioned before, always call the specific airlines or charter group that will be flying you to your destination about their bike policy. The answer you will usually get is that your bike can be checked as part of your luggage. Also, most airlines today will require that you prepare your bike for the flight. This usually means making the bike less bulky and more portable. To do this, deflate your tires; remove both pedals; and loosen the expander bolt on your handlebars, and turn them to the side. Lastly, remove your front wheel, and strap it to the bike frame. Put the pedals in your pockets or hand baggage and carry them on the plane. (Watch out for the metal detectors!)

Even better is to get a box from a local bike shop and pack your bike in that, making sure to mark your name and address clearly on the outside. This will protect your bike from careless baggage handlers and will most likely make the airlines happy as well. For a small fee, some airlines will even provide you with a carton.

THE BIKE TRAIN

Trains, in general, are kinder to bicyclists than airplanes, especially in Europe. In the United States, the national train line, Amtrak, does have a policy but not many of the company's employees seem to be aware of it, which means you could have a few problems.

In general, Amtrak will take your bike on a train as baggage in a separate baggage car, but they require that you check the bike in a day before you plan to leave and usually suggest you put it in a carton for its own good. A wise idea since Amtrak does not reserve a separate section of its cars for bikes. The charge for this is a few dollars.

Life for the train-traveling bicyclist is a little easier in Europe. Usually the only precaution you take, even when traveling with your bike, even to another country, is to remove all bike bags; remove the bike pump; print your train destination on a slip of paper, and attach it to the bike with tape (or slip it in the spokes); and then check it in at the baggage counter. For a long train journey, it's not a bad idea to check in an hour or so before your train departure to increase the odds of it getting on the same train with you. Except in Britain, where you can take your bike on a train free of charge (apart from the morning and evening rush hours) the fees charged are nominal. Usually the bike will travel on the same train as you do, or it may come a little later on another train following yours.

BUSING YOUR BIKE

Another alternative for the traveler in the United States is shipping your bike by bus by one of the two national bus lines, Travelers or Greyhound. As long as you neatly carton your bike, Travelers will accept your bike as baggage and carry it on the same bus as you. Greyhound is fussier. It also requires you to put your bike in a carton but charges you extra to ship it because it considers the bike freight, not baggage. The charge is by weight and distance. Also it will drop it off only in cities where it has facilities for handling package service. Lastly, Greyhound recommends that you arrive an hour before departure to check in your bike.

TOURING THE UNITED STATES: GENERAL INFORMATION

This and the following sections will offer suggestions on where to go and how to get there. For most countries, the suggestions will be a week-long trip. The one exception to this is the United States. There's too much to see and it's too vast to cover with a single suggestion. But if you're considering a tour in the United States already, you probably also have some inkling of where you'd like to go: the South, Northeast, the Midwest, the Southwest, the Northwest, or the West Coast. Each area has its own particular appeal—the rolling hills of Vermont in the Northeast, the wide open spaces of the Midwest, the scenic, rugged coastlines of the Northwest.

Probably the two most complete sources of information on tours all over the country are American Youth Hostels and Bikecentennial.

American Youth Hostels

American Youth Hostels (AYH) has local chapters scattered all over the United States. They offer bicycle tours for all range of riders, from the inexperienced to the experienced, and have tours lasting from 2 to 6 weeks. Don't be thrown by its name. Adults as well as teenagers and children are active participating members. Information on joining AYH, or about local chap-

ters offering tours of interest to you, can be had by writing the organization's national office. (See Appendix for address.)

Bikecentennial

Bikecentennial is an American bicycling organization set up in 1976, the year of the United States bicentennial, to promote bicycling all over the country. It's most famous for having mapped out a scenic 4,450-mile (7,160-kilometers) route for bicycles that meanders across the United States from Oregon to Virginia. It has more recently charted local scenic routes in the states of Virginia, Kentucky, and Oregon. You can sign up for guided camping tours of all or part of this coast-to-coast route or local routes and get full information by writing to them at their headquarters in Montana. (See Appendix for the address.)

Maps

For touring on your own, you may not need set tours, but you will need maps. One good source in the United States is Bikecentennial. You can purchase from them map booklets laying out in elaborate detail every part of its cross-country route complete with topographic detail and information on everything from campgrounds to

The broken lines show the cross-country route for which Bikecentennial has detailed map booklets.

grocery stores. You can get a complete set of five booklets for the whole cross-country run or just one book for the stretch you want.

Bikecentennial is also in the process of mapping routes through some of the national parks. Information about these maps is available by writing the organization's headquarters.

For areas not covered by Bikecentennial, there is another map source: the United States government, specifically the U.S. Geological Survey (USGS). Relying on sharp aerial photos, this agency has mapped the entire United States in exhausting detail. Depending on the scale of the map, you can find elaborate topographic detail complete with local landmarks and even small back streets. The scale best suited to the bicycling tourist is the 1:250,000 series in which 1 inch (2½ centimeters) on the map represents about 4 miles (6 kilometers) on the ground. For their quality, these maps are not all that expensive.

To order the ones you'll want, you have to know the right map number and have the appropriate form. An index of the maps and the forms are available free from one of two USGS offices. (There's one for states east of the Mississippi and one for those west of the Mississippi. The addresses are given in the Appendix.) When you write for the index, make sure you specify the 1:250,000 series, which has its own separate index.

TOURING EUROPE: GENERAL INFORMATION

When it comes to information on items such as the locations and prices of campgrounds or even getting maps to plot a trip in Europe, a good start is the national tourist office of the country you plan to visit. Beyond that, you will probably want maps and guides of your own.

Camping

For camping, one of the most convenient general guides is a thick paperback book called *Europa Camping and Caravanning*, a multilingual guide to campgrounds all over the continent. It's available both in Europe and the United States. If you live in the United States, a useful book is Rand McNally's *European Campgrounds and Trailer Parks*, which lists over 3,000 campgrounds in Europe.

Maps

Road maps for France, Switzerland, Germany, Italy, and Holland are available from Michelin. This company's maps are extremely clear and useful. For the United Kingdom—England, Scotland, Wales, and Northern Ireland—the Scottish map firm Bartholomew has good maps. (See the Appendix for addresses of both companies.)

Guidebooks

In addition to its maps, the Michelin company offers a wide line of guidebooks for its mother country, France, which are as detailed as you could want. Most famous is the red book called the *Guide Michelin*, which names and rates some of the top restaurants in France and gives you valuable information on local sights all over the country. Almost as handy is the compact green booklet *Camping Caravaning en France*, a multilingual guide to campsites all over the country.

Other Ideas

Some countries, Great Britain and the Netherlands in particular, have bicycle-touring groups that will provide you with maps, hook you up with tour groups, and even map routes for you in some instances. For England, the organization to contact is the Cyclist

Touring Club (CTC). (See Appendix for address.) This organization offers services such as maps, route planning, and guide books.

In the Netherlands, the Royal Dutch Touring Club (address in Appendix) is also a good source for maps of the bicycle paths that vein that country.

SPECIFIC EUROPEAN TOURS

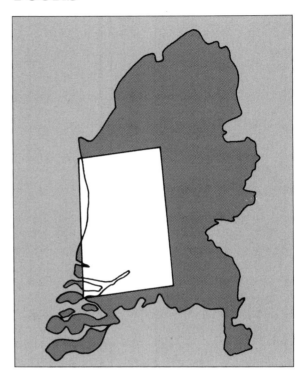

THE NETHERLANDS

Because its topography is very, very flat and because it pays deference to bicyclists (they have their own lanes and traffic lights), the Netherlands, or Holland as it is sometimes known, is paradise for the cyclist. As you travel, you'll see many bikeways marked two different ways. One type will have a round blue sign with a white outline of a bicyclist on it. Both bicyclists and moped riders must use this path and not ride in the road. The second type is a path with a black rectangular sign reading "rijwielpad" or "fietspad" in white letters. This path is restricted to bicyclists only or to moped riders who ride with their engines off, and its use is optional.

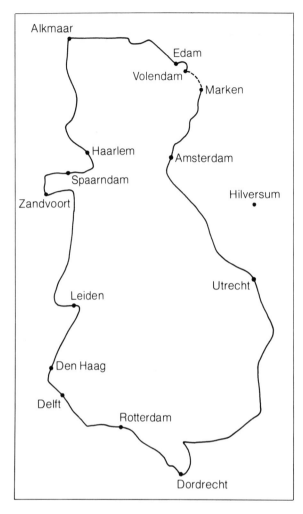

Amsterdam-Utrecht-Amsterdam

MAPS: Michelin Map No. 408, or those supplied by the Royal Dutch Touring club. (See Appendix for address.) Local maps can also be had at area VVV or Tourist Information Offices in the Netherlands.

DISTANCE: Approximately 177 miles (285 kilometers)

This tour concentrates on the west of the country and includes the coast as well as most of the major cities worth seeing. Fortunately for the cyclist, you can see a lot of the Netherlands on this tour, although by no means all of it. The next time you visit,

you can try the less heavily industrialized north where the picturesque West Frisian Islands are located.

This route will hardly cut you off from nature, however, since Holland has some 200 miles (320 kilometers) of coastline to satisfy your craving for time on a beach. Nor will you feel cut off culturally. The Dutch are multilingual and so, in the larger cities at least, the chances are that if you speak German, French, or English, language will not be a problem. The climate is also as welcoming—mild summers with cool mornings and evenings, especially by the sea. So, take a warm sweater even if you plan to travel in midsummer.

DAY ONE: Amsterdam to Alkmaar (29 miles/48 kilometers)

If you're going to do the rest of your trip on schedule, you'll have to use a little self-restraint in limiting your sight-seeing around Amsterdam. The range of sights is broad, from the Rembrandt masterpieces in the National Museum to Anne Frank's house. Head north out of the city by taking the ferry from the Ruyterkade behind the Centraal station. Once you've crossed over, follow the road to Monnikendam, continuing on to the showpiece island village of Marken. You can hop a ferry there that will take you on to the town of Volendam, a fishing village whose inhabitants wear folk costumes (not for the tourists, but because that's the way they live). Just north of there, a ferry from Volendam will take you to Edam of cheese fame but also noted for other sights such as the fine stained-glass windows on its seventeenth-century church. From there follow the roads west to Alkmaar, which has a colorful cheese market every Friday (May through October). If you miss the market, you can still see some of Alkmaar's sixteenth-century architecture.

DAY TWO: Alkmaar to Haarlem (24 miles/40 kilometers)

You can then amble down the coast, cross the canal locks, and head to the town of Spaarndam, where you can see a monument to the legend of Hans Brinker, who is famous for saving his country by putting his finger in a hole in the dike. From there you can turn east to tulip country (bloom time is April and May) and to the town of Haarlem. Even if there are no tulips, you'll find there the Frans Hals Museum, cafes to relax in, and crafts shops where you can buy gifts.

DAY THREE: Haarlem to Leiden (27 miles/44 kilometers)

Pedal east and then south to the popular North Sea resort Zandvoort and then start heading back inland and follow the road to Leiden. This will take you through, among other places, the town of Keukenhof, famous for its floral displays in season. Once you get to Leiden, you'll find many lovely old houses in this town where some of the great painters of the Netherlands—Rembrandt and Jan Steen to name two—were born. If you really want to see local color, take a trip to the west of town and have a look at the fish and eel market.

DAY FOUR: Leiden to Delft (24 miles/ 40 kilometers)

Just down the road from Leiden is the city of Den Haag, where the seat of government for the Netherlands is found. It's a picture-postcard city full of parks, beautiful examples of fourteenth-, fifteenth-, and sixteenth-century architecture, and impressive buildings such as the Peace Palace, built around the turn of the century. Just outside of town is the popular tourist attraction of Madurodam, a knee-high, miniature Dutch village. Continue 5 miles (8 kilometers) east of Den Haag to the town of Delft, probably best known for its painted pottery but also in itself a restful place with tree-lined canals to visit.

DAY FIVE: Delft to Dordrecht (20 miles/32 kilometers)

Not too far down the road is the city of Rotterdam, the Dutch city that boasts the largest port in Europe and the second largest in the world. You can take a boat tour of the docks or explore on your own. The city is a phoenix since it rose from its own ashes when the Dutch rebuilt it after it was totally destroyed in World War II. Travel 15 more miles (24 kilometers) down the road and you'll find the picturesque river town of Dordrecht. It's one of the oldest in Europe and an ideal place to wander and let your curiosity be your guide. It's an old European town in the most charming sense.

DAY SIX: Dordrecht to Utrecht (29 miles/48 kilometers)

From Dordrecht, head west and then north towards Utrecht, a town divided in two by a canal. You approach it across a wide open plain and cross two rivers—the Lek and the Waal—to the south. The city itself is a pleasant surprise: part of the town is still intact from the fourteenth and fifteenth centuries. For a better view of the surrounding countryside, climb the tower of Utrecht Cathedral (nearly 370 feet/ 112 meters high). For those who are precious-metal minded, there is also a gold and silver museum.

DAY SEVEN: Utrecht to Amsterdam (24 miles/40 kilometers)

Before you reach Amsterdam, you will pass through Hilversum, a spectacular new town in the country and a showpiece of modern architecture surrounded by a lush countryside. It's worth a stop if you have the time.

Note: although this is broken down as a 7-day trip, you may find it possible to do it in fewer days, as you will the other trips described in this chapter.

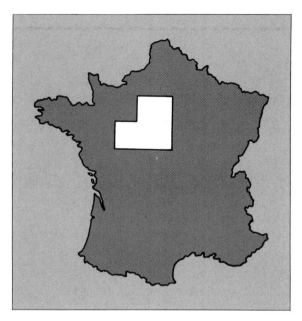

FRANCE

Ask anyone who has traveled extensively in France for a single recommendation of an area to tour on your bike and you are more likely to be given a list. The variety of terrain and cultures in France has contributed much to its allure for tourists—from the rugged Pyrenees and Alps in the southwest and southeast to the green rolling hills of Burgundy and the tropical beaches of the south of France. The range of choices is tremendous.

To give you help with that choice, the Michelin tire company has produced a small library of travel aids on France. These are guides for specific provinces, campground guides, the famous restaurant guide and, best of all, their maps. Especially valuable is the so-called 1:200,000 series in which the mapmakers have divided the whole country into a grid of finely detailed maps that not only give you a detailed layout of secondary roads, but have an added unique feature as well—they also show the steepness of the hills using small chevron symbols. One chevron on a road is the sign of a slight grade—9 percent or less—and it ranges up to three chevrons—for a steep 13 percent (or more) grade. Not only will you not get lost with these maps, but you will also be able to plan the best hill-free route possible.

The Chateau: Paris to Saumur

MAPS: Michelin Maps Nos. 60 and 64
DISTANCE: Approximately 215 miles (345 kilometers)

It's hard to reduce France to one tour, but for the sheer spectacle of both scenery and architecture, the chateau tour along the Loire River southwest of Paris is at the top of most people's lists. The area is studded with beautifully maintained castles that belonged to the nobility in the

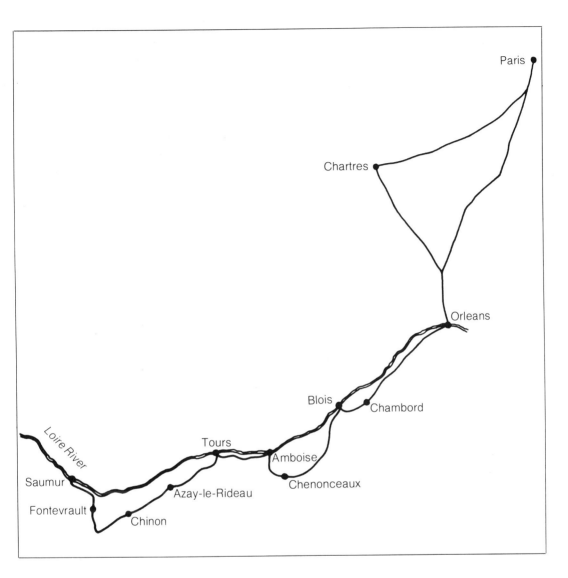

fourteenth and fifteenth centuries and, as a boon to cyclists, has a network of quiet back roads that roam through the heavily wooded river valley. It's a memorable trip.

DAY ONE: Paris to Orleans (45 miles/ 72 kilometers)

Well worth a visit, if you can manage it, is the stunning Notre Dame cathedral at Chartres, which some claim to be the most beautiful in the world. It's a classic of Gothic architecture: a world-famous stained-glass window and ornately decorated entrances that are masterpieces in themselves. It's just a 1 hour train ride from Paris, so you can save your bicycling energy for later on. From there, Orleans is a long but easy bike ride (45 miles/72 kilometers), so give yourself plenty of time. If you don't have time for Chartres, you can take a train straight to Orleans and start your tour there. The site of Joan of Arc's victory, Orleans is an important commercial center perched on the banks of the Loire. It's a good rest stop to collect your energies for your trip down the Loire valley.

DAY TWO: Orleans to Blois (35 miles/ 56 kilometers)

Cross the Loire and head west down the road toward Chambord. On the way you'll pass the Chateau d'Avaray, four ghostly towers left standing from its former days of glory. Not too far from there is the masterpiece of the Loire valley, the Chateau Chambord. This is the largest of the chateaux, an immense place of 440 rooms that suddenly appears at the end of a long avenue. If you can manage to arrive at sunset, it's worth it. Just a short distance off the river road (make a left at Muides), it's situated in a large park that's ideal for exploring by bicycle. Continue down the road about 12 miles (20 kilometers) and cross the river to Blois. Up on a tall hill you'll find the Chateau Blois looking down on the river and the town.

DAY THREE: Blois to Chenonceaux (31 miles/50 kilometers)

Cross back over the river on route N764 and follow the road to the next chateau at Chenonceaux, the star of the tour. As soon as you come upon it, you'll see why. Built right on the Cher River on a series of stone arches, the mansion also has a castle keep and a meticulously kept garden. The chateau itself is also known as the Chateau of Six Women, after the six women who played important roles in it throughout its 400-plus year history. Among them was the famous Catherine de Medici who gave spectacular parties in this still spectacular place.

DAY FOUR: Chenonceaux to Tours (31 miles/50 kilometers)

Head back toward the Loire River, crossing at Amboise where part of the chateau commissioned by the fif-

teenth-century French king, Charles VIII, still stands. Charles was only 13 years old when he commanded that the fortresslike chateau be built. The place is full of history: it was where Leonardo da Vinci spent his last days and, on a more grisly note, where French Protestants were bloodily executed in the sixteenth century. When you cross the river and travel west, you will be pleasantly surprised by Tours, a half-old-half new city partially rebuilt since World War II. There is no chateau here but there is an old part of town dating back to the fifteenth century that is worth exploring.

DAY FIVE: Tours to Fontevrault (42 miles/67 kilometers)

Cross to the other side of the river and follow the road west to Azay-le-Rideau, a quaint old town with its own chateau and inviting winding streets. Continue down the road until you get to St. Maure, where you'll take a right and head northwest to Chinon, which has a mammoth castle-chateau overshadowing the riverside town. It has an authentic old quarter that will take you back to the Middle Ages. Backtrack slightly to the main road and head west to Fontevrault, which contains a beautifully reconstructed abbey with some original and bizarre architectural touches.

DAY SIX: Fontevrault to Saumur (30 miles/48 kilometers)

Head west to Saumur, the end of your journey. There you'll find shooting straight up out of a rocky promontory the local chateau, a fortress really. In its long history, this fortresslike chateau was a nobleman's house, a governor's residence, a prison, and a barracks, and today it has evolved into a museum.

SWITZERLAND

It would be stretching the truth to say that Switzerland is an easy country to cycle tour. It has the Jura Mountains in the west and the Alps in the east. But inbetween Switzerland also has some beautiful lake country with a liberal sprinkling of immaculate towns and villages.

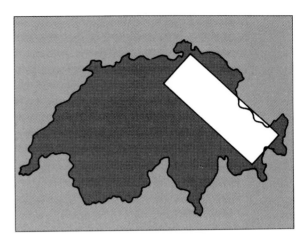

Still, you can't be in Switzerland without being too far from the mountains, and even if you're a cyclist, you shouldn't try to avoid them all because the climb up them by bike is well worth the scenery once you reach the top. To give you a taste of both the flat and mountainous Switzerland, we've put together this civilized tour of the midlands and the east, beginning in Zurich. Don't feel as though you should pedal every inch of the way. If at any time the hills get too much for you, you still have the alternative of public transportation, usually not far away. The country is well serviced with a network of train lines that are fast, extremely punctual, and kind to bicyclists.

Zurich to St. Moritz

MAPS: Kummerly & Frey (see Appendix for sources); Michelin 1:200,000 series (set of four for Switzerland).

DISTANCE: Approximately 119 miles (190 kilometers)

DAY ONE: Zurich to Zieglbruke (36 miles/60 kilometers)

This casual ride will take you along the south shore of Lake Zurich from the largest city in Switzerland, which is a smooth blend of the old and the new in both customs and architecture. You have an option of a variety of routes to take. Most direct is route 3, which hugs the shore of the lake and will show you some nice scenery and some local traffic as well. For a short scenic diversion, you could follow route 4 out of town and at Adiswil

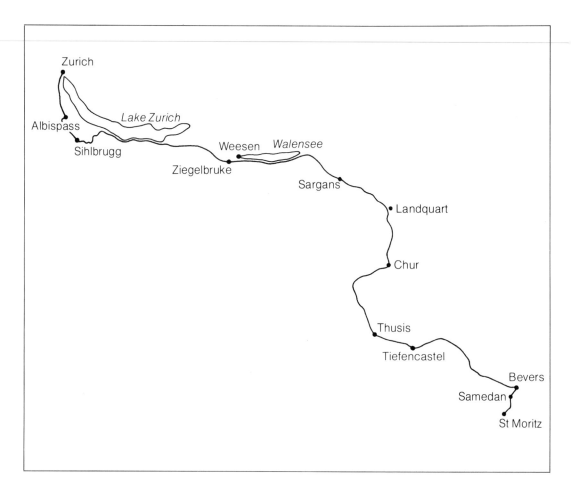

take a right toward Langnau for a scenic push over Albispass. At Sihlbrugg you then have a variety of routes back to route 3 and the shore route, which eventually will lead you to Ziegelbrucke. In one day you can get a taste of both the lake and the mountains.

DAY TWO: Ziegelbrucke to Chur (36 miles/60 kilometers)

As you leave Ziegelbrucke, the scenery becomes more mountainous and more spectacular as the road snakes past the Walensee and the small resort town of Weesen perched on the far western end. Follow the road (easy enough to do since it's the only one)

southeast towards Sargans and continue on passing Bad Ragaz, a spa whose water is brought down to it by aqueduct; Landquart; a number of nameless castles perched on the side of the mountains; and finally the provincial capital of Chur in the heart of the Alps.

DAY THREE: Chur to Tiefencastel (25 miles/42 kilometers)

From Chur head east until you reach Heichenau, and there turn south towards Thusis, a small crossroads resort in the mountain valley. Here you will face a moment of truth as a bicyclist. Mountains and mammoth climbs lie ahead. If you're an experienced and adventurous cyclist, you could ride on following the Abula River to Tiefencastel, or if you'd just rather look and not ride, take a train to the next town. Either way, your reward will be a spectacular panorama of Swiss mountain scenery.

DAY FOUR: Tiefencastel to St. Moritz (22 miles/36 kilometers)

As the crow flies, it's not that far from Tiefencastel to St. Moritz, but the terrain is mountainous and you will have to decide whether to take the train over the hard but scenic mountain route to St. Moritz, or take the train. One word of advice, unless you've brought plenty of warm clothing, it might be wise to take the train. Midsummer snowstorms are not unknown in the mountains and aside from that, evenings and mornings can be extremely chilly. You might want to save your strength for exploring the hiking trails on the peaks around the fashionable resort village of St. Moritz or for a short bike trip down the road to the town of Samedan where, among other things, you can be taken for a ride in a glider by one of the local soaring pilots. If you do decide to ride, take the road heading west out of Tiefencastel toward Surava. Follow it over the mountains to Bever and then head southwest towards St. Moritz.

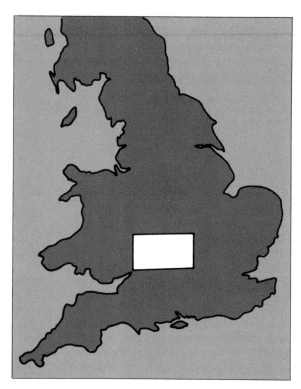

ENGLAND

England is one of the world's premier cycling countries. Awaiting the cycle tourist there is a superb network of secondary roads. The traffic on secondary roads is spare and slow. The people are extremely polite, helpful and—most important—accustomed to cyclists. The bicycle is a popular means of transportation, and few innkeepers will be surprised by your arriving on a bike. And finally, the country is simply beautiful. The English countryside doesn't have the breathtaking scale of, say, the American West or the grandeur of the Alps. But what it has is an intimate, quickly changing terrain that's almost tailor-made for cycling speed. You can be pedaling through rolling hills, then half an hour later cruising over meadowland, then into wooded areas, and perhaps even passing near a seashore, all within one day's ride.

Most of the country is suited to cycling, with the obvious exceptions of industrial cities such as Birmingham, Liverpool, or Manchester. East Anglia, the southeast section of England (and the old Saxon kingdom) is a good area for beginners. It is the flattest part of the country and relatively untouristed. A busier area is central England, which features Stratford-on-Avon and Shakespeare country. A favorite area for cyclists (and everyone else) are the southwest shires of Devon and Cornwall. Devon is perhaps Britain's most popular holiday county, with its valleys and rolling hills and villages of cob and deep thatch. The area is also known for its good food. Cornwall is right next door, but it's wilder than Devon with weather-beaten cliffs and coves along its long coastline.

Also popular is the Lake District in the northwestern corner of the country. It's scattered with lakes and

Chipping Campden

Broadway

Moreton-in-the-Marsh

Chipping Norton

Stow-on-the-Wold

Kingham

Charlbury

Bourton-on-the-Water

Burford

Cirencester

mountains, but while the countryside is beautiful, the cycling can be strenuous and disconcerting to novices because of the number of tourists and motorists wedged into this small area in the summertime.

The Cotswold Roundabout: Charlbury to Kingham

MAPS: Bartholomew half-inch series: Nos. 18, 19, 14 and 14 and Ordnance maps (see text)

DISTANCE: Approximately 78 miles (125 kilometers)

Bartholomew has divided England into a series of detailed map grids, some 60 individual maps that show in minute detail main and very lightly traveled roads as well. In addition, through the British Tourist Authority you can get even more detailed (and more costly) ordnance maps that cover England, Scotland, and Wales with 200 individual maps. They are about twice as expensive as the Bartholomew maps, but worth the money. These maps give you not only the names of towns and roads but also the names of farms and groves, and in addition they even point out fences, ruins, and footpaths.

This tour is perfect for beginners who have not yet mastered the traveling skill of always having a place to stay at night when they stop. The trip only requires that you know how to use a telephone and how to make reservations at one of the many B&B's (Bed and Breakfasts—inns that are often private homes as well) in the Cotswold area.

Once the great wool center of the thirteenth century, the Cotswolds, which lie about 75 miles (120 kilometers) northwest of London, have a tremendous number of B&B's as a byproduct of it's being a popular tourist area for years. As an added bonus, the area is evenly dotted with towns so that as you follow this circular route, you will never be more than a short day's ride from three or four other towns, and also, of course, from a choice of accommodations.

The tour mapped out here is only a general guide. Follow it according to your whimsy and curiosity. The Cotswolds are so richly veined with back roads that you might find it fun to start making up your own tour after you get situated. Traffic is always light or practically nonexistent on these roads (unless you also count the sheep you'll meet), and the countryside is unspoiled.

One last point. Distances listed are approximate. There are a dozen ways to get from one town to the next, so don't be misled by what appear to be low figures. By taking some more meandering side roads, it would not be all that difficult to double the distance given for a part of the tour. This tour is for 5 days, but if you want to take a longer trip, don't worry about getting bored. You can crisscross the Cotswold area for at least a month but yet you will never see the same road twice.

DAY ONE: Charlbury to Burford (10 miles/16 kilometers)
Charlbury is a little station town just a few railroad stops from Oxford. It's less than a 2-hour trip from London's Paddington Station. Begin your stay in the Cotswolds by pedaling the short trip to Burford. You'll pass through Wychwood Forest and over the Windrush River getting there. Burford is the main commercial and shipping town of the Cotswolds, and a good place to stock up on any items you forgot at home, such as maps. It has plenty of good inns, and if they're full, try the beautiful towns of Swinbrook or Minster Lovell just to the east.

DAY TWO: Burford to Cirencester (30 miles/48 kilometers)
You could stretch this ride to double the distance or more if you wanted to, there are so many things to see between the two towns. On your way out of Burford, visit the Cotswold Wildlife Park, an open-air zoo without the crowds and the stench of most zoos. It has a good collection of the little-seen red pandas. Also be sure to pass through Bibury, which poet William Morris called England's most beautiful village (in fact, you may want to spend the night there instead of Cirencester). Cirencester itself is an old Roman town, whose former importance as the chief wool market you can gauge by the fact that five main roads converge on the town like spokes on a wheel.

DAY THREE: Cirencester to Bourton-on-the-Water (20 miles/32 kilometers)
There are countless different routes you can take between these two towns, but try to pass through Chedworth Woods on the way. Bourton-on-the-Water is a very popular tourist town, and it may make sense to call for reservations a few days in advance, or

to stay at nearby Upper or Lower Slaughter.

DAY FOUR: Bourton-on-the-Water to Broadway (20 miles/32 kilometers) You'll want to keep the distance down on this leg because you'll be passing through five great towns: Upper and Lower Slaughter, Stow-on-the-Wold, Moreton-in-the-Marsh, and Broadway. Your destination, Broadway, is the most famous of all Cotswold towns and the most touristy. If this bothers you, you may want to bed down in one of the four previous villages. (Those interested in Shakespeare country should be aware that Stratford-on-Avon lies only 15 miles/24 kilometers miles to the north.)

DAY FIVE: Broadway to Kingham (25 miles/40 kilometers) This final leg leads you through the two Chippings—Chipping Campden and Chipping Norton. Campden is known for its beautiful old Market Hall and Norton for its tweed mills. Just a short distance from the latter is Kingham railway station, where you can catch a train that will take you back to London; or better yet, stop off in Oxford for a few days.

Chapter 6

RACING

Did you know:

• That for several years during the 1970s an international poll confirmed that the world's most popular athlete was not Pele, or even Muhammad Ali, but a man few Americans have ever heard of—Eddy Merckx, a bicycle racer from Belgium?

• That the drug scandal of the 1978 Tour de France, while shocking so many people, is nothing new to cycle racing? Drug-taking has been an almost integral part of racing, and one of England's greatest cycling heroes, world champion Tom Simpson, actually died in the 1967 Tour de France due to a drug overdose.

• That professional bike racers average over 25 miles (40 kilometers) per hour, even in races of 100 miles (160 killometers) and more, and that cyclists make demands on their bodies more brutal than in football, soccer, or hockey? For instance, one veteran time trialer explained how he knows when to ease up: My body tells me if I'm overdoing it, he says. When the blood from his lungs starts flowing up into his mouth, he knows that it's time for him to slow down.

• That American women cyclists have brought home many more world championship medals during the 1970s than American men have, and yet have received little or no support from United States bicycle racing organizations? While heralded in Europe as super athletes, women such as world champions Sheila Young and Sue Novara remain relatively unknown in America.

• That one of the most revered athletes in Europe at the turn of the century was a track racer named Marshall W. Taylor? He was considered by many to be the fastest sprinter ever to ride, and he's still remembered by cycling enthusiasts in France. No doubt you have never heard of Taylor. But the reason you haven't is not because he was a Frenchman. He was an American. And he was black.

THE RACING SCENE

There are always things to criticize about every sport. And bike racing has had its share of scandals—fixed races, payoffs, and especially drug scandals. Although such things are not to be excused, professional racing (even amateur racing) involves a lot of pressure and a lot of money. To win, some people will do whatever they feel is necessary. Why drugs? Because, in truth, they sometimes help. Some racers allegedly take stimulants to allow them to push to top speed again and again throughout a race. Some may take steroids to build up muscular development and for endurance through the long season. Some take megadoses of vitamins. Some have even reportedly used blood doping. That is, they have a pint of their own blood extracted during the winter off-season and then have it re-injected before a race to give them an extra oxygen supply. The racing season is long and tough. Imagine the Tour de France—2,000 to 3,000 miles (3,200 to 4,800 kilometers) over 21 days. Then dozens more of 100- to 200-mile (160- to 320-kilometer) races from early spring to late fall. Some racers may feel they need an extra lift to get through it all. Drug taking is obviously dangerous, illegal, against the rules, and guarded against by officials. But it undoubtedly still happens.

To European racing fans, such news is no great shock. But Americans may find it unsettling because bike racing is still a fresh, new innocent sport in the United States. But the United States has its problems, too, albeit of a different nature.

What we have in America is a rampant amateurism that is grossly frustrating to our serious riders. The main racing organization in the United States is called the United States Cycling Federation (USCF). The name was changed recently from the Amateur Bicycle League (ABL) to get away from the "amateur" label. Well, the name has changed, but many racers feel the old spirit remains. The USCF, like the ABL, has a habit of suspending the very best racers in America for the strangest of reasons. The USCF, for instance, does not like riders to raise their arms at the end of a winning race. This, believe it or not, can be cause for suspension. Some racers have complained that officials have even tried to interfere in their personal lives. And then there's the case of the women.

During an 8-year period from 1968 through 1975, American women won six world championship medals, while their male counterparts collected a grand total of one. Yet world sprint champion Sheila Young (also a world and Olympic champion speed skater) complains that she had to pay her own way to Europe in order to compete in the world championships.

Still, even though the powers-that-be in the United States sometimes act foolishly, the important folks—the racers—are a fascinating group to know. And bicycle racing—amateur or professional, European or American style, riding yourself or just spectating —is definitely worth trying, especially if you like the feel of a fast bicycle under your body.

WHAT IT TAKES

The speeds attained in bicycle racing are fantastic. Let's say you want to try bike racing. Begin by choosing a 20-mile (32-kilometer) course for yourself and riding it, in one hour flat. You can do it? Great, that's a 20-mph (32-kmph) ride, and not bad for a beginner. Now do it eight more times in succession, with no rest periods. That's 180 miles (288 kilometers) at a 20-mph (32 kmph) pace. Sound impossible? Well, that's how far professional cyclists rode at a recent world championship road race, except they averaged a blazing 27 mph (43 kmph).

This is not meant to discourage you. You don't have to pedal at 27 mph (43 kmph) in order to compete. Obviously, there are lower levels of competition—bike clubs at the local level, for instance—that provide races for the less-than-superathlete. But be forewarned that racing is not just touring at a fast clip. It's serious stuff, and the people you'll meet in racing clubs are liable to be grim folk, at least when behind the handlebars. Should you decide to give racing a try, it's best to find a club where you'll get help and advice from fellow members on how to train and how to race. (Local clubs throughout Europe and America are obviously too numerous to name here, but these clubs can be easily found by inquiring with your local bike store owner—particularly if the owner specializes in racing equipment.)

Training demands lots of hard riding. Finding the time to put in lots of miles—say, a few hundred per week—is difficult for many people. But perhaps even more of a problem is the hard riding. Many people who consider themselves physically fit are not accustomed to really pushing their bodies, especially joggers and recreational cyclists. These are people who are in fact "fit." But not in a competitive sense. They find no problem running 10 miles (16 kilometers) a day, or even bicycling 100 miles (160 kilometers) or more a day regularly. But racing requires you to sprint at times, and that means grabbing those handlebars until your knuckles turn white and thrashing your legs up and down with all the violence you can muster for several minutes at a time.

What many racers do in training is something called *intervals*. That is, they pedal along easily, then explode and sprint as fast as they can; then slow again, then a sprint, then slow, and so on. This is realistic exercise because it's often the way races are run, with cyclists making a break for the lead or trying to step up the pace at various times as part of some intricate strategy.

Those high speeds mentioned earlier shouldn't intimidate you too much, for two reasons. First of all, they referred to world-class professionals. Amateurs go slower (though not much slower). And second, there's a trick to it. The trick is called *sitting in*, a drafting technique which in part explains the high average speeds attained in bicycle racing. This is the basic tactic of almost all bike racing, and it involves tucking your bike directly behind another rider. Any cyclist moving faster than 10 mph (16 kmph) creates a wind-broken pocket of still air directly behind his or her rear wheel. And if you "get on his or her wheel," the lead rider will break the wind for you and cut your effort by about 15 percent.

Sitting in is the primary tactic around which overall strategies are based, and as such it presents delicate problems and decisions for every rider. Staying in the middle of a group of cyclists, for instance, is obviously less taxing than going out in front and breaking the wind, leaving you more energy for the final sprint to the tape. But you might also get trapped in the middle of the *peloton*, as it's called, and never get your sprint off. Or, oftentimes a cyclist with great endurance, but less sprinting power, will make a breakaway. He or she will go out in front alone, hoping to build up an unbeatable lead. Then riders in the peloton have to come to an unspoken group decision on whether to pick up the pace or not. A group of two or more riders may decide the peloton is not going fast enough to catch the breakaway and set out on a chasing party. If these cyclists belong to the same team, they will cooperate with each other and take turns leading while the others draft behind. In fact, even racers from competing teams, or racers riding solo, may come to an unspoken agreement to share the lead in order to catch a common enemy, the breakaway cyclist.

Then again, a chasing party may include a rider who blatantly does not cooperate. Say three cyclists leave the peloton, either to catch a breakaway or to form a cooperative breakaway of their own. Two of the riders exchange the lead, but the third refuses to get in front, continuously drafting behind the other two and conserving his or her strength while they use up theirs. The other two are then faced with a decision. Do they continue the breakaway? They've already expended valuable extra energy getting away from the pack. But if they continue "towing" their uncooperative partner, he or she will be fresher and perhaps will outsprint them at the finish. So, should they step up their pace in hopes of losing their uncooperative partner, or slow down and let the peloton catch up so they can get a rest?

If you think this sounds complicated, there are even more factors that come into play. The cyclists must further consider the motives of the other riders. Perhaps the third "lazy" cyclist is a teammate of the racer who made the lone breakaway. Perhaps it is the "lazy" cyclist's intention to convince the other two to give up their chase

just by sitting in behind them and enjoying a "free" ride. All these speculations are what make bike racing not only a physical sport, but an intellectually stimulating experience as well.

KINDS OF COMPETITION

There are two basic kinds of competition in cycle racing: road racing and track racing. *Road racing* is done on a 10-speed ultralightweight bike over conventional roads that may have been blocked off to motor traffic for the duration of the race. *Track racing* is done on an oval track with a fixed-gear, or track, bicycle. This is a 1-speed bike with no freewheel (it cannot coast) and no brakes. It is a stripped-down machine, meant to go very fast and that's all.

The various types of races in road racing and track racing and the rules under which they're run are discussed in the following sections.

Road Racing

Road racing is the most popular kind of cycling competition, and it usually attracts the most people—both participants and spectators. And it's probably the fastest human-powered method on earth of moving from point A to point B.

The three most common types of road races are the following: long road race, the criterium, the stage race, and the time-trial race.

Long Road Race. The *long road race* is not a standard length. How long it is can vary from 10 miles (16 kilometers) for very young riders, age 9 and 10 for example, to well over 100 miles (160 kilometers) for adults. However long it is, riders usually complete it in a few hours at the most. For example, in the United States the road-racing championship covers a 120-mile (192-kilometer) route that top competitors will cover in a little over 4 hours.

For all the different types of road races, cyclists use a 10-speed ultralightweight bike with modified features to suit each particular event.

Criterium Race. More specialized than the long road race is the *criterium*, a shorter race that is usually run on a closed course between 1 mile (1.6 kilometers) and a ½ mile (0.8 kilometer). Unlike the long road race, it is less a test of stamina and more a test of riding skill. Riders travel a total distance of anywhere from 20 to 50 miles (32 to 80 kilometers) in a series of laps that run over a course that usually features some tricky turns and maybe a hill or two, which keep the course interesting.

Because the race is relatively short, riders worry less about stamina and more about speed and bike-riding strategy. The criterium is one of the bike racing fans' favorite races because it's on a small scale—a large part of the race can be seen from one viewpoint—and with a good field of competitors, some real finesse in riding style, and possibly some spectacular pile-ups as well can be seen. Being able to hit and hold high speeds and keep a good position on tight corners are two of the challenges the criterium rider faces. Spectators often cluster near some of the more dangerous or challenging parts of the course just to see how well or poorly their favorite riders perform.

One thing both the long road race and the criterium have in common is that in a field of mixed riders, the racers may get handicaps: that is, the race may use a staggered start—letting the slower, less experienced riders go first—to even out the odds a little more. One difference between the long road race and the criterium is the bike used. Long road racers use a bike that resembles a touring bicycle; that is, one with a springier frame, able to take and absorb the abuse of hard riding for more than 100 miles (160 kilometers). Criterium riders don't travel as far and need a lighter bike, one with a stiffer, more responsive frame, more closely resembling the lines of a track bike.

Stage Race. The *stage race* is one of such tremendous length that it has to be run in stages, or segments, usually over a period of several days. It offers the challenge of both the long road race and the criterium, plus much more. The stage race is the ultimate challenge for the racing cyclist because it not only demands enormous stamina—probably more than any other athletic event—but also often incorporates in it elements of other races, such as the criterium or the time trial, which will be discussed later. Usually the winner is decided by a point system. Riders are awarded a certain number of points according to how they finish at the end of a day's ride or how they place in certain tough stretches of the race.

Although there are stage races held all over the world, every cyclist and racing fan agrees that the ultimate stage race is the Tour de France, run every summer through the French countryside and occasionally threaded through neighboring countries on the way to the traditional finishing point in Paris.

Mapped out every year by the French sports journal *L'Equipe*, the route varies in length from one year to the next, but always runs well over 2,000 miles (3,200 kilometers) long and takes anywhere from 20 to 25 days to complete. France has all kinds of terrain and weather, from the mountains and snow in the southeast to the torrid tropical temperatures along the Mediterranean, and the routes sample a little of each.

It's the ultimate bicycle race. Only the best riders in Europe, which is to say the world, qualify to compete—just being in the field of the Tour de France is an honor—and of those only a portion finish. It's not unusual to see as many as a third of a field of hardened, experienced riders drop out before they ever see the finish line in Paris. It is the ultimate test of physical stamina in cycling, and probably in all athletics. For a cyclist to win a Tour de France is to achieve a level of popularity only a handful in world athletics ever realize. Five-time winner of this grueling event, Eddy Merckx, was earning close to half a million dollars a year by the time he retired from racing.

During the 3 weeks it runs, close to a third of France turns out to watch the racers at different points of the route, and the progress of the favored riders monopolizes sports pages all over Europe. And short of all-out nuclear war, there is little else in the way of news capable of eclipsing the event.

Time-Trial Race. All the road races you've read about so far are different in many ways, but they do have two things in common: they are usually massed-start events; that is, a crowd of cyclists gather at the starting line and take off all at once; and the racers are out there on the road with a competitor they can see. The one road race that has neither of these elements is the *time trial*, in which individual riders or teams of riders race against the clock. They are never on the road at the same time as their competitors, and they depend totally on themselves for motivation to win. The winner of this event is the rider or team of riders who completes the course in the shortest amount of time.

It's an exhausting event. Riders have to pedal at top speed for the entire course, which typically measures 10 miles (16 kilometers) or 25 miles (40 kilometers). To make the event even more challenging, some racers tackle the *hillclimb* version of the time trial which, as its name suggests, is run up a particularly steep and/or long hill and demands tremendous mental and physical stamina.

Track Racing

More specialized both in equipment and the demands in rider skill and equipment is track racing, so-called for the obvious reason that it's done on a track that, from above, looks like a large oval bowl with sloping sides. There's a bewildering variety of track races; we will cover only some of the most popular.

Match-Sprint Race. Easily the most popular race in track is the *match sprint* in which just two riders compete in a test of nerve and skill over a 1,000-meter course. The rider who crosses the finish line first is the winner, but the race is not that simple.

According to the rules of the match sprint, only the last 200 meters of the race are timed, so that riders with the best times will compete with each other in later races. The first 800 meters is a nerve-wracking cat-and-mouse game in which the riders jockey for position. To the first-time viewer, a match sprint race will look something like this: A starting gun is fired and the two riders barely move. For a long time they'll poke along around the track, constantly staring back and forth at each other and trying to get in each other's way. Usually one rider moves out in front slightly, but not too far or too fast. And this rider spends most of the time staring over his or her shoulder at the competitor. Then when the race seems almost over, the two riders will turn on the speed, pedaling in a frenzy for the finish line. Then the race is over.

In the match sprint, riders use the first 800 meters simply for jockeying into a good position for making the final burst for the last 200 meters. Different riders have different styles. Some prefer to be in front so that they can block the second racer and have a clear track ahead when they want to make their moves. Others prefer the rear position because it gives them the advantage of getting the jump on the lead rider when he or she isn't looking. In races where both riders prefer the same position, either front or rear, you'll see a lot more jockeying, each trying to force the other rider into the less-favored position. Riders know when they've reached the sprint area because a bell goes off 200 meters from the finish line.

Life then gets more complicated. The sprint part of the race lasts just seconds, but in those few moments there's a tremendous burst of energy —and sometimes violence. In the excitement of the chase, or just as a matter of cold-blooded racing tactics, bicyclists have been known to elbow or sideswipe an opponent to win. Elbowing and sideswiping are, of course, illegal, but it happens.

The track bike has no freewheel and no brakes. It is extremely light and is designed for the short, sharp bursts of speed in competition track racing.

Physically, the ideal sprint racer is short and compact, with thick, powerful legs. In addition to power, this racer has fast reflexes that give him or her the ability to jolt from a slow pace to a blinding sprint. Psychologically, the star sprinter should be blessed with the killer instinct, the ability to take advantage of any mistake or any hesitation by the opponent.

Pursuit Race. At the start of the *pursuit* race, which can be a confusing event to watch the first time, two opposing riders are poised on opposite sides of the track and try to catch each other by riding over a distance of anywhere from 3,000 to 5,000 meters.

Since, usually, this type of thing will only happen in the most unevenly matched races, the winner is usually the rider that finishes the course in the fastest time.

A variation on the pursuit is the *team pursuit* in which two teams of four riders each race under the same rules. This is an elegant event to watch because different riders take turns pacing the four-person teams, which ride in single file to minimize air resistance. At different points in the race the lead rider drops back and lets the racer behind lead for a while. This spreads out the work of pacing the pack a little more evenly.

When done well, the changing of the leader is an amazing thing to see. The leader speeds up a bit, climbing slightly up toward the top of the track. The three riders behind slip by and at the right moment the old leader drops back in place behind the third rider. Only the best cyclists can orchestrate this move smoothly. To do it well requires superior team coordination, the result of long hours of practice, and a keen sense of timing.

It's important that the team ride together as closely as possible since the race time is taken when the second rider of the team crosses the finish line.

Kilometer-Time-Trial Race. Probably the most exhausting of all track events is the *kilometer-time-trial* race in which a racer simply pedals as fast as possible for the entire 1,000 meters. Out on the track alone, the racer's opponent is time. In many ways it's a hybrid event since it calls for the speed and explosiveness of a sprinter but also requires the staying power of a good distance rider.

Six-Day Race. Not every bike race ends up on the Olympic roster. One track event that was created in England but reached its heyday during the Great Depression in the United States is the *6-day race*, also known as le Madison, after Madison Square Garden in New York City, where it often took place. Originally the event was a marathon bicycling event in which one bicyclist rode around and around a track for 6 days and nights (or as long as possible). Sunday was a day of rest, so the race had to end on a Saturday. The fastest survivor was the winner.

The modern, more civilized variation is also run for 6 days, but two riders compete as a team and only ride for about 2 hours each of the 6 days.

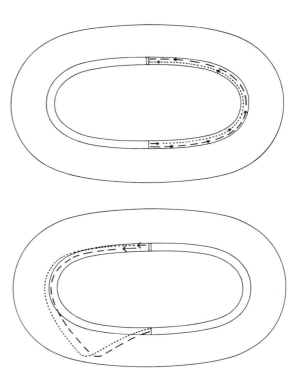

In track racing, such as the match sprint races shown above, tactics are of the essence. Nearly all begin with the riders jockeying, almost at a standstill for second place from which they can see the other rider and time their final sprint exactly. In many cases, one or both riders will use the banking of the track to try to beat the other in the final sprint.

Rules and tactics vary, but generally only one rider of a team races at a time. The team with the most points, scored on periodic sprints run throughout the race, or with the highest number of strong finishing leads of a lap or more, wins the event.

A 6-day race is a crowd pleaser of an event, particularly when riders change places, which happens every few laps. At a prearranged time the replacement rider, who has been slowly circling the racing pack, will speed up and drop down into the race. As the replacement rider does this, the partner, who is dropping out, grabs the replacement rider and literally flings

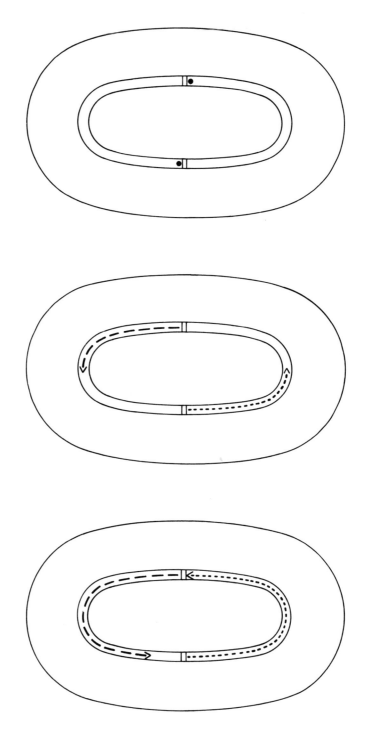

The pursuit race is the easiest event for beginners to enter: though it demands speed and discipline, the skills it calls for are basic enough to be learned fairly quickly with steady practice. Riders begin on opposite sides of an oval track and race to their opponents start line.

him or her into the race, a move known as the "Madison sling." Sometimes this is done just by one rider grabbing the other rider's arm. More often, riders wear special racing shorts with a handle built right into the side that the other rider can grab.

Motor-Paced Race. Just as peculiar is the *motor-paced race* in which a field of track racers known as "stayers" each ride behind a specially equipped motorcycle. It's rigged so that the motorcycle driver can stand up as he or she drives, thereby acting as a human windshield for the cyclist who follows close behind. At the back of the motorcycle is a small roller so that if the cyclist's front wheel should accidentally bump the motorcycle, he or she won't go down.

The bicycle racer has to pedal fast enough to stay inside of the protective air pocket created by the motorcycle ahead. By shouting commands, the rider can get the pacer to speed up or slow down as the rider's race strategy dictates. Whatever the rider does, he or she can't fall too far behind the pacer or the turbulence just outside the protective air pocket would knock the rider over in a second. Since motor-paced riders routinely hit speeds of 50 miles an hour (80 kmph) or more during this event, the effect would be devastating.

Cyclocross Racing

One last oddity of bike racing is *cyclocross* racing. The best way to describe it is as a combination of cross-country racing and running an obstacle course while carrying a bicycle that may occasionally be ridden. The course is not a long one, but it takes the rider over a route that no bike was ever meant to follow—over fields, down and up valleys, and across streams.

The cyclocross racer uses a sturdy 5-speed bike equipped with special knobby tires and short pedal cranks for ground clearance. On a good course, the competitors may actually be riding the bike only about half the time. The rest of the time they're running with the bikes slung over their shoulders. It's a muddy, messy event that draws its fair share of enthusiastic masochists.

RIDER STYLES OF ROAD RACERS

As you probably already suspect, there's much more to racing than just being able to pedal fast. This is particularly true of road racing, a complex and demanding sport. And since that's where you are most likely to get your preliminary racing experience, it is the best area on which to concentrate.

To be a good road racer you have to have an overall strategy, and this means that you must know your strong and weak points as a rider. Road racers typically fall into three groupings: gimpeurs, or hill climbers; sprinters; and rouleurs or pacers. Of course, life isn't this simple. You may have more than one bicycling talent, but most likely one will dominate.

Gimpeurs

Of the three styles of riders, *gimpeurs*, or hill climbers, are the most specialized. The strong point of gimpeurs is pedaling up hills at a rate that leaves most of their competitors gasping and staggering all over the road. Hills are the places where gimpeurs can make their moves and gain a little on the pack. So the hillier the course, the happier the gimpeurs.

The rest of the race can be a problem for gimpeurs because typically they are tall with long, lean muscles. While their large size is no liability on a slow uphill stretch, it can be a problem going down the other side because their large bodies make for increased wind resistance, a factor that makes them work harder, especially if there is a strong headwind.

Sprinters

Wind resistance is not a problem for *sprinters* because this kind of rider usually has a short and powerful build like good track racers. Their talent is for the abrupt, fast breakaway and the quick reflexes and killer instinct that lets them use it to good advantage.

Typically the riding strategy of sprinters is to hang with the pack as best as they can, sprinting ahead when they think it's possible to gain and hold a decent lead. Or, they may hang back until they near the finish line and then use their sprinters' prowess to burst by the leader before anyone knows what has happened.

Rouleurs

Much more understated is the riding style of *rouleurs*, or pacers. They don't have the power to pump up steep hills nor the quickness to make threatening sprinters. What they do have is amazing stamina. They try to set a pace that few other riders can handle. In fact, a good pacer or a group of pacers can actually control a race— burning out the hill climbers long before they reach a hill and forcing the sprinters to use their energies before they get within threatening distance of the finish line.

Pacers also have to know their own weak points. If they set too fast a pace for themselves, they might use up themselves before they can make their own breakaways and try for the finish line. That kind of knowledge comes with experience.

TACTICS FOR ROAD RACING

Let's assume for the sake of argument that you've done all the right kinds of riding and practice with the advice of a good coach and are ready to take part in a road race. Your coach will no doubt give you some good advice, but just to give you an idea of what's involved in preparing your mind for the race, here are some basic suggestions on how to approach the event.

The Race Course

First of all, get to know the race course. If possible, ride over it and get a feel for the topography, road surface, and even the road width. It can all make a difference when you know what's coming up. Pay extra attention to the last stretch of road near the finish line. Most likely this is where you and many others will be making your big move. Check for any potholes, sandy patches, anything that could spell disaster to a frenzied sprinting cyclist not watching where he or she is going.

Pay attention to other environmental details. At what point will prevailing winds be blowing with or against you? What are the roads like? Are they clean? Do they have any patches with a brick or cobblestone surface? Try out the hills at a racing tempo to see just how hard they are. Keep your eyes open and remember what you see.

Finally, know who your opponents are. Find out what riding styles they prefer. Try to match their styles with the various stretches of the road you just covered. This should help minimize at least some of the surprises as you ride.

The Start

At the start of a race, try to get as close to the front of the pack as possible. You won't be able to choose your pace crammed in the middle of a crowd of struggling riders. It can also be a little dangerous to ride too far back in the back, especially on downhill runs. The reason is that if one rider goes down, he or she will probably also take down a few other riders who are immediately following. By staying ahead of the pack instead of with it, you can avoid joining this group accident. For that reason, it's a good idea to practice getting off fast from a dead start. It will come in handy at the start of the race. Don't let the fact that there will be dozens of other riders trying to do the same put you off.

During the Race

As you get off, try to find a rider that best approximates your riding tempo and keep with that person. Ride his or her wheel for a while if you can get away with it, or at least try to match the pedaling tempo to carry you for a while. Always make sure to avoid the side of the road no matter how you ride. It's too easy to get boxed in when you're way over to the side, and there is the added danger of more debris and an unpredictable road surface.

At the same time, don't get caught towing someone else unless it's by arrangement. By riding in front, you're breaking much of the wind resistance for him or her, giving that person an easier race. It does happen with racing teams that some members are assigned to tow the star rider within striking distance of the finish line so that the star can conserve his or her strength for the big sprint to victory. Unless this is your job, don't make life easier for any other rider.

Hills

Hills sometimes break many riders' spirits and permanently throw them off pace. You can avoid some of the heartache by taking it easy up a big hill if hill climbing is not your strength. Once again, find a rider whose pace you can match and use that rider to lead you up the hills. If you can manage it, try to stay in the front of the pack once you reach the top. Don't be first, however. Hang back

a little. Let a couple of other riders sound out the road ahead of you. On a steep downhill run you could be hitting fairly high speeds, and one surprise pothole at high speed could wipe you out for the rest of the race. Keep away from the main pack because, as mentioned before, in a crowded pack when one rider falls, so do the many riders behind.

Also, make the most of your downhill runs. Too many riders slacken up once they hit the top of the hill. For the first part of the ride they might even sit and coast for a short while before pedaling again. Don't get into this habit. Take the opportunity to build up momentum once you've passed over the crest. Make gravity work for you. Give a couple of strong pedal thrusts to get yourself going and watch some of the lazier riders in the race fade away.

The Finish

As you approach the finish line, positioning and timing are critical. You should be a little off to one side of the road, not so far over that you could get boxed in, but far enough to keep an eye on your competitors by looking over one shoulder. That way you should be able to see who is making a sprint for the finish and who is watching you. Some riders will tip off their planned sprints when they reach for their shifting levers to change gears or hunch over into a more streamlined position on the bike.

If you want to panic the other rider into sprinting earlier than they should you should try to force them into making a move. Go through all the motions of reaching for your gears and changing position and hope that the rider is so jumpy they automatically begin a breakaway attempt...and exhausts themselves before reaching the finish line.

The secret to really making a good sprint is to do it as unobtrusively as possible. Some riders even have their shifting levers installed in the ends of their handle bars so that they can shift without moving their hands too far and tipping off their sprints.

Lastly, concentrate on the finish line and aim the end of your sprint for some point beyond it. That way you can protect yourself against the photo-finish effect when you let your effort slacken off just enough at the end to let another cyclist sneak by and win by just a hair.

TACTICS FOR TRACK RACING

To really learn anything as a track racer, you have to get a bike and get out on a track and ride. Riding with a good racing club helps. Only after you've been riding with them a while will any of the following tips be useful.

If there is no track near and it doesn't look like track racing is in your future, you still might want to look over this section since it will make you a more intelligent bicycle-racing spectator and give you some useful insights into the sport.

Track racers are different animals from road racers. Ideally track racers are powerful and fast, capable of pedaling at high rpm's for short stretches. They can take off from a dead start at amazing speeds and have extremely fast reflexes.

In the match-sprint race, one of the riders has to take the lead, something predetermined by drawing straws. Since some racers don't like being in front, they may roll a few inches or centimeters over the starting line, to satisfy the letter of the law, and then stop dead, trying to force the other rider ahead. Most riders don't want to use their explosive starts until they're within striking distance of the 200-meter mark and finish line.

Then there are those who can do a long-winded sprint, and their main tactic is to pin the trailing rider to their right, high up on the lip of the track. They keep their back wheels between their opponent and the bottom of the track and use an elbow to prevent him or her from slipping by on the right. When the time is right, they can then drop down the sloping track and make their sprints for the finish.

Short-winded sprinters prefer to keep their opponents trapped in the lower part of the track, especially if the opposing rider is long winded. To win the race, they depend more on quickness than stamina. The idea is to shoot up toward the top of the track as fast as possible and then use the momentum as they come roaring down the sloping track to get a jump.

As in road racing, sometimes a long-winded sprinter will fake a surge of power to trick the other rider into making his or her move too soon. Another may try a bicycling tactic called *surplace*. This tactic involves stopping the bike by backpedaling slightly and actually balancing in place, rocking the pedals back and forth like a unicycle rider. This very often happens at the beginning of the race when a rider who drew first position tries to trick the other rider into going past him or her. It's a tricky balancing act and one that is tough on the leg muscles. This usually falls in the domain of the more experienced cyclist.

As mentioned, jockeying for position takes up most of the first part of a sprint race. Most riders prefer second place for a number of reasons. By tagging along close behind the first rider, a cyclist can take advantage of the hole the other rider has punched through the air and pedal with less wind resistance. The second rider can also keep track of what the opponent is doing, unlike the first rider who must keep looking back to see where the enemy is. And even if the number two rider should get pinned in by the first rider's wheel, he or she can get free by cutting the pace slightly and then letting the opponent pull ahead by just a little.

The other kind of race you are most likely to encounter is the pursuit event in which two riders chase each other around a track starting from opposite sides. Tactically this is a much simpler race than the sprint. While sprint racers eventually wean themselves from road training and spend as much time as they can working out exclusively on the track, good pursuit riders divide their time between the track and the road. The pursuit race demands more stamina since a cyclist has to ride a much longer distance.

Pursuit riders do miles and miles (or kilometers) of road riding to build up their stamina and leg power, maybe even practicing on long hills to get themselves in shape.

Tactics of pursuit riders fall into two general categories. One is simply to climb on a bike and pedal like a maniac for the entire race, which could run for as long as 5,000 meters. Since few people have this kind of stamina, many riders save their bursts of speed for the last 1,000 meters and turn the last part of the event into an elongated sprint.

These are just a few glimpses of what bicycle racing is all about. Bike racing cannot be summed up in one chapter of a book because it's a complex sport. It has a rich and glorious history. It has dedicated athletes, pushing themselves to the limits of human strength, endurance, and pain. It also has an inglorious side of drug-taking, even by the high and mighty. It has big money, six-figure salaries and profitable product endorsements for some, and tales of no money at all for others, even world champions. And it has speed and tactics and danger and breakneck treks through exotic lands. In short, bike racing has everything that makes life interesting, heartbreaking, and dramatic.

Chapter 7

MAINTENANCE MADE SIMPLE

This chapter is for people who like to ride bicycles, not fix them. Your first objective should be to avoid doing any repairs at all. And the two most common problems—flat tires and rough-running moving parts—can be held to a minimum with a little preventive maintenance, outlined below.

AVOIDING FLAT TIRES

Always inflate your tires to the proper pressure (often stamped on the side of the tire). Don't overinflate as this could be risking a blowout because the inner tube will be stretched beyond its capacity. A more common problem is underinflation—a careless cyclist is apt to pedal off without bothering to put a gauge on the tires before a ride. Many tires, especially the higher-pressure models, can lose appreciable pressure in a week or even from day to day; underinflated tires cannot tolerate bumps, rocks, and other road hazards. You can always safely inflate your tires to the maximum, except when it's over

80 degrees Fahrenheit (26 degrees Centigrade) outside, in which case it's better to reduce by about 5 pounds (2 kilograms) to allow for heat expansion.

To avoid punctures, of course you should avoid riding over sharp objects or patches of broken glass. But the biggest threat is not a tack or other sharp object immediately piercing the tube as you ride over it. More common is a piece of glass or smaller fragment sticking to the tire and working itself in as you ride—perhaps not puncturing the tube for dozens of miles. Therefore, brush off the tire treads from time to time with a gloved hand as you ride, or stop and carefully clean them occasionally.

CLEANING AND OILING

Rough running is a problem that develops gradually. Your wheels don't spin as they once did; nor do your handlebars feel quite as fluid; the chain starts making dirty crunching noises; and your gear shifters begin to balk more and more every week. What has happened is that your bike has become dirty. Road grit has infiltrated the moving parts and everything just naturally gets sluggish. Not only that, but the dirt displaces the lubrication —oil and grease—that made your bike such a slick running machine when you first bought it.

Cleaning

Make it a practice to wipe off the chain after every day's ride. You can rub as hard as you want to get rid of the grime. Don't worry about the fact that you're also removing lubricant. Any grease on the outside of the chain is useless—it just collects dirt. The only lubricant doing any good is on the inside surfaces, in the rivets, plates, and rollers. This is also true for the other parts of the bike. While it's not necessary to clean other parts after every ride, as with the chain, you should occasionally wipe dirt away from the wheel hubs, pedals, brakes, derailleurs, bottom bracket, and so on. In short, clean in the very same places where you lubricate.

Oiling

Do not oil every time you clean the bike. Every couple of months should be enough, if the bike rolls well and all the moving parts do their jobs without creaking, or squeaking, do not oil it. If you must err, err on the side of too little rather than too much lubrication because extra oil just attracts more dirt. When you do lubricate, do it sparingly. A couple of drops of light bicycle oil will do for each part (as shown in the illustration). After oiling, wipe dry again.

The arrows indicate the crucial points that require lubrication. Light oil lightly spread is what you should use: be careful not to over-oil your bike. Too much of a good thing is almost as bad as none at all as oil can attract grit and dirt.

TOOLS NEEDED

There are dozens upon dozens of bicycle tools; and some of the most expensive ones perform only a single esoteric operation. We don't advise buying such tools until you absolutely need them. But here are seven common tools that will get you through about 90 percent of the repairs in this chapter. It's unlikely that you'll live through the lifetime of your bike without needing each of the following:

• *Pressure gauge.* Don't try to judge whether your tires are properly inflated just by looking or feeling. You can be off easily by 20 or 30 pounds (9 or 13 kilograms). And that can be the difference between a safe bike and a blowout or a flat. Just as there are two kinds of tires, clinchers and sew-ups, so there are two kinds of gauges, Schraeder and Presta. Schraeders are for regular clincher tires; Presta for sew-ups. Be sure you get the right kind for your bike as they are not interchangeable.

• *Screwdriver.* you may already have one of these. One with a ¼ inch (½ centimeter) blade will do.

• *Pliers.* Handy for brake repairs and all sorts of other tasks, but don't use your pliers instead of a wrench for turning nuts or bolts because that will round their heads.

• *Crescent wrench.* Sometimes called an adjustable wrench, this tool will be your workhorse. Buy a good one.

• *Vise-grip.* While not totally necessary, this tool is useful to have around. It's a type of very strong pliers with a spring inside that allows you to clamp it on a nut or bolt and lock it in place. This frees both your hands to work elsewhere. You can use a vise-grip in place of pliers in any of the repairs discussed here.

• *Tire irons.* Usually sold in sets of three, these are small metal pries used for taking clincher tires off the wheel when you have a flat. (Only one iron is illustrated, but you'll need all three.) A warning: There's always a temptation to make your screwdriver double as a tire iron. Don't. The screwdriver's sharp edges could rip the inner tube. If you have sew-up tires, you won't need tire irons.

• *Oil.* A small can should do. There are also many space-age substitutes for oil sold in bike stores—gels, sprays, and other forms of bicycle lubricants. These are fine, but then so is good old oil.

• *Miscellaneous.* Of course, you'll need a tire pump, rags, and a patch kit for repairing flat tires. You should also have some way of hoisting your bike off the ground so that you can work on the wheels more easily. A special rack is nice, but ropes or hooks suspended from a garage ceiling or tree also work.

And an almost essential "tool" is a can of special hand cleaner—the type used by garage mechanics for wiping off grease.

REPAIRING CLINCHER TIRES

As explained in Chapter 1, bikes are equipped with one of two kinds of tires: sew-ups or clinchers, which are more common. Because you are more likely to have to change a clincher tire, this type is discussed first.

To save yourself a little time and aggravation, don't assume that every flat tire you get is the result of a puncture. If you leave your bike unused in a corner all winter and take it out for that first spring ride only to find what appears to be a flat tire, it's very possible all the tire needs is a little air. No tire is absolutely air tight. They all lose a little air every day, and over a period of weeks or months they

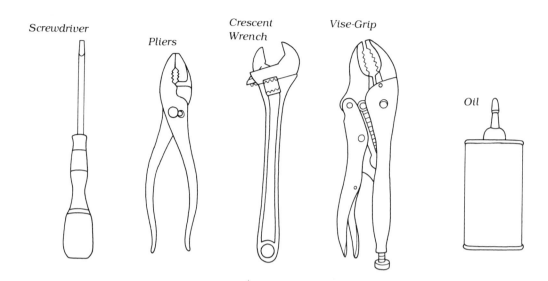

Screwdriver   Pliers   Crescent Wrench   Vise-Grip   Oil

You'll be able to take care of the majority of bike repairs with one or more of these tools.

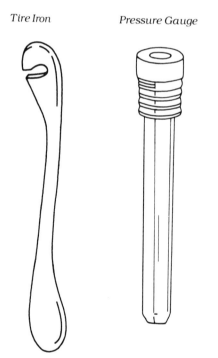

Tire Iron   Pressure Gauge

can gradually go flat. Get out your pump and reinflate the tire. Wait an hour or so and go back and check. If it's still nice and hard, your tire doesn't need any more attention.

To repair a clincher tire, you'll need the following items: bicycle pump, crescent wrench, tire irons, tire pressure gauge, a replacement tube, and a tube repair kit (for your flat tube).

Removing the Wheel

No one has yet figured out a way to fix a flat tire without getting the wheel off the bike, so right away you face your first mechanical challenge.

Front Wheel

Look at where the front axle is attached to the bicycle frame. All 3-speed bikes and 1-speed bikes usually have two nuts holding the axle. Bikes with 5 speeds or more may have either nuts, wing nuts, or quick-release levers holding the wheel in place.

If you have nuts on your axles, simply get out your crescent wrench, adjust it to the nut size, and loosen the nut on either end of the axle. With a little nudging, the wheel should then drop out.

If you have a bike with center-pull brakes, you'll have to flip up the quick-release lever on the brakes to open them so that you can pull the wheel free. And if wing nuts hold the axle in place, you can usually loosen these with your hand. Or if you have quick-release levers, the job is even easier. Simply pull on the lever so that it is pointing straight out to the side and then slide your wheel free.

Rear Wheel

If you have a 1-speed bike with a coaster (or back-pedal) brake, the first thing you should do is unfasten the small metal arm attached to the bike frame. Then use your wrench to loosen the nuts on the rear axle and remove the wheel.

If you have 3-speed bike, you should first shift your gear changer into third, or high gear. Now follow the cable back to where it connects with a short chain leading directly into the center of your rear hub. At the end of the cable is an adjusting sleeve—you'll recognize it by its knurled surface. Unscrew this counterclockwise until it's free of the chain leading into the hub. (See illustration under "Fixing a 3-Speed Shifter," page 117.) Once the cable is free, loosen the nuts on the axle and lift the wheel out.

For anyone with a 5-, 10-, or more-speed bike, getting the back wheel off is a little trickier. Before you do anything, shift your gear changer so that the chain is resting on the smallest rear gear. And if you have center-pull brakes with quick-release levers, flip the levers to open the brakes wider. Now loosen whatever is holding your rear wheel to the frame. If there are nuts, use a crescent wrench. If there are wing nuts or quick-release levers, you can use your hand.

To remove the wheel, stand behind the back wheel of your bike so that you're sighting up the length of it. Hold onto the frame with your left hand, and with your right hand, reach down and grab the rear derailleur. It's spring loaded, so you can pull it back toward you. Do this, pulling it back as far as you can. This will give the axle a little more clearance so that you can get the wheel out.

To free the wheel, give it a little nudge with your knee. If you're lucky, this will knock it free of the bike frame. If it doesn't, give it a harder nudge. (Don't get discouraged if you have a little trouble at first. After a while you'll get the knack.) That should loosen it enough so that you can pull the wheel free of the chain.

Removing the Inner Tube

To remove the inner tube you use the tire irons as miniature crowbars to pry the edge of the tire off one side of the rim. Take one iron and slip the blunt end, the end with no notch in it, under the edge of the tire (as shown in the illustration on page 108). Bend the tire iron down, and hook the notched end on a spoke to hold it in place.

Leave that there, and take out a second tire iron. Not very far to the right of the first iron, slip the blunt end under the edge of the tire, and pry it up as you did before. This should slip some of the tire over the edge of the rim. If the tire pops back onto the wheel, take that second iron, pry up the tire edge, and hook the iron onto another spoke as you did with the first one.

Once you've pried the tire loose over the edge of the wheel, continue prying it free with a third iron moving slowly and carefully around the rim until one side of the tire is completely hanging over the outside of the wheel. Once that's done, you can then remove all the tire irons.

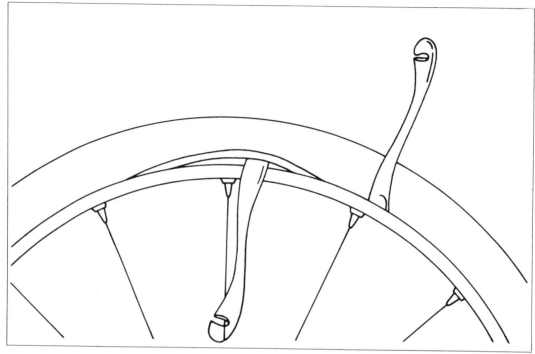

To repair clincher tires, you'll need a set of tire irons to deal effectively with the task of removing your flat tire from its rim.

Next, reach inside the tire and start pulling the inner tube out where you can see it. Don't take it off the wheel yet. Leave it attached where the tube valve pokes through the hole in the rim. Get your bicycle pump, and pump up the tube until it's fat.

To check for leaks, look at the valve first. Put some spit on your fingertip, and rest it lightly on the top of the valve. If bubbles start puffing up around your damp finger, that's a sign you have a faulty valve. If that's the case, the tube is not worth repairing.

If the valve seems fine, listen for the hiss of escaping air and slowly run your hand around first the outer and then the inner perimeter of the tube. You should be able to feel the puff of escaping air and find the leak. Circle the spot with a piece of chalk.

Before you remove the tube, look closely at the area where it touched the tire or rim. If the puncture is on the outside perimeter of the tube, check the tire in that same area for nails, bits of glass, sharp wires, or even a sharp pebble that may have penetrated. If you find anything, pick it out at once, otherwise you might get a flat tire with the new tube as well. If the puncture is on the inner perimeter of the tube, take a very close look at the points where the spokes poke through the inside of the rim. Only the spoke nipples, which hold the spokes in place, should be exposed. If you see the end of the spoke poking through, get a metal file and smooth off the tip of the spoke. Then, pull the tube completely off the wheel. (Sometimes you might have to unscrew a small metal collar at the base of the valve holding it onto the wheel.)

Replacing the Inner Tube

If you plan to use a brand new tube, you'll have to pump a few puffs of air into it first so that you can work with it easily. Don't put in too much air, just enough to separate the insides, which might be stuck together.

To begin, take the valve of the tube, and poke it through the hole in the rim designed for that purpose. Now, working away from the valve on either side, tuck the tube up into the tire and on the rim using your hands. To replace the tire, do the same thing, slipping it on the rim with your hands working away from the valve as you go. At first, this will be easy, but as you get to the end, you may not be able to squeeze the rest of the tire on the rim with your hands. If so, take a tire iron and using the blunt end, pry the rest of the tire back onto the rim. The most important thing is to make sure that the tube is not pinched between the tire and the rim anywhere on the wheel. Never use a screwdriver to poke the tire or tube back on the rim, as you could easily cause another puncture and have to start all over again.

Repairing the Tube

Properly repaired, an old inner tube will be almost as useful and as durable as a brand new one. Always make it a habit never to travel any distance without a tube repair kit handy. Typically, a kit will contain some glue, a small swatch of sandpaper, or something to roughen the tube, chalk, some rubber patches of different sizes, and often one large piece of rubber patch material that you can cut to suit your own needs.

There are times when you shouldn't even bother trying to repair a tube: when the hole in the tube is more of a gash or when the puncture is near the base of the valve. No tube repair kit can fix these satisfactorily. Your best bet is simply to throw the tube away.

If you decide to make a repair, first pump up the tube so that it is one and one half to two times normal size. That should stretch it enough so that you can locate the puncture in nine out of ten cases. For that one out of ten, hard-to-find puncture, fill a pan or wash basin with water, and rotate the tube through it until the hole, which will be spewing out bubbles under water, makes itself known. Mark the puncture spot with a pen or piece of chalk, and get out the tube-patch glue and a rubber patch.

Select a patch large enough to cover the puncture area and about a ½ inch (1 centimeter) of surrounding rubber as well. Make sure the punctured area is clean, and if your kit includes a small swatch of sandpaper or a small piece of metal with an abrasive surface, use it to roughen the area you plan to patch. This will help the patch adhere to the tube much more tightly.

Take the tube of glue that comes with the kit, and squeeze out a small blob of glue, and spread it around the area to be patched. There should be enough glue spread around to equal the size of the patch you will use. Once you've spread the glue, set the tube aside, and wait about a minute, long enough for the glue to dry a bit and get a little tacky.

All tire patches have an adhesive backing and some kind of backing paper over that. Remove the paper and be careful not to touch the sticky back of the patch as you do. Position the patch over the glue-smeared area, and press down hard with your hand for about 10 to 20 seconds.

Replacing the Wheel

To replace the front wheel, simply slip the axle into the notch at the end of the forks, center the wheel between the forks, and tighten in place. Again, if there are nuts use your wrench. Otherwise you can use your hands to tighten the wing nuts or retighten your quick-release lever. When you tighten your quick release, make sure to press it down. It's less likely to get snagged on something and pop loose. If you also have quick-release brakes, make sure you retighten them so that your brakes will work.

To replace the rear wheel on a coaster bike, slip the chain back onto the chain sprocket, slip the axle into the slot in the frame, center the wheel, and tighten the axle nuts with your wrench. Then your final step is to reattach the coaster brake arm to the bicycle frame.

To replace the rear wheel on a 3-speed bike, slip the chain back on the sprocket, and guide the axle into position making sure you center the wheel before you finally tighten the axle nuts. Lastly, after double checking to make sure your gear selector is in third, or high gear, screw the adjusting sleeve on the end of your gear-selector cable to the chain leading into the hub. Spin the small locknut against the adjusting sleeve to hold it in position. Pump up the tire, and check the air pressure to make sure it is properly inflated.

For 5- or more-speed bikes, slip the chain back over the smallest sprocket. If you have a quick-release lever on your hub, hold onto the lever and first loosen the cone-shaped nut on the other side of the axle to make it a little easier to slip the wheel into position. Pull your rear gear changer or derailleur back toward you and slip the wheel axle into the slot for it. Be especially careful to get the right side of the axle as far into the slot as it will go. It may take a little time and a little wiggling, but be patient. It will go, eventually.

Once the wheel is in its notch, retighten the cone-shaped nut on the hub the same number of times you loosened it. Center the wheel between the chain stays on the bike frame, and push the quick-release lever down toward the ground. If it's well adjusted, it should be a little difficult to push it the last fraction of the way. Lastly, don't forget to reset your quick-release brake levers if you have them, and pump the tire to the right pressure.

REPAIRING SEW-UP TIRES

As with clincher tires, you'll need a pressure gauge and pump—but of the Presta variety to repair a sew-up tire. You won't need tire irons, but you will need rim tape or glue (available in most bike stores). Removal and replacement of the wheel is the same as described in the previous section.

When your sew-up tire goes flat, remove the wheel and strip off the bad tire. Starting with the side away from the valve, gently peel the tire off the rim. It should come off easily. A sew-up tire can be patched, but it usually isn't worth doing. If you wish, buy yourself a special tubular tire patch kit. Most will have instructions included, which will inform you that you must unsew the tire casing, patch the leak in the tube inside, and then resew the tire. It will tell you how to do these things in Italian, French, and maybe—but not always—in English. And even should you do this procedure successfully, patched sew-ups have a tendency to rupture again rather quickly, and most experienced cyclists use them only for local riding.

The safest solution is to discard the tire and put on a new one. The first step is to remove the old rim tape, which should strip off easily. If the old tire had been held to the rim with glue, you'll have to remove it with some type of solvent. Now apply fresh glue or rim tape. The glue is probably safer because it should hold a little better than the tape. And when going around a sharp corner at high speed, you'll feel more secure knowing that there's less chance of the tire coming off the wheel. However, if you don't intend to race or ever go fast around corners, you can get away with the tape, which is much easier to apply and remove.

Run the tape around the entire circumference of the rim, starting and ending at the valve hole. (But don't cover the hole up; the tire valve has to stick through there.) Make sure you get the tape squarely on the rim edge, with none creeping over the sides where the braking surfaces are. This is an even bigger problem with glue, which you can apply with an old toothbrush, but a bare fingertip is probably more accurate.

First, stretch the new tire out a bit by hooking it over your knee and pulling hard. Stretch it at several points around its circumference so that it is evenly loosened up.

Insert the valve through the hole in the rim. Working away from the hole, push the tire onto the rim—hard! Depending on the tire, this can be very difficult to do. If you can't get it on, try stretching the tire again. You can get some leverage by setting the wheel on the ground to give you something to push against. But make sure it's soft ground so that you don't misshape the wheel. Also be aware that you may be picking up some dirt or grass on the rim tape or glue that you'll have to remove just before slipping that final few inches of the tire over the rim.

Now look back at the valve to make sure it's at right-angles to the rim. If it isn't you'll have to take the tire off and start again. If the valve isn't straight, it means the tire is unevenly tensioned and could wear down the tube near the valve and cause a flat. Once you get the tire on properly, inflate it slightly, just enough to give it some shape. Now you'll be able to see whether the treads are straight. Shift the tire around on the rim until they are. You'll be able to do this easily because of the low amount of air pressure in the tube and because it takes a while before the rim glue or tape and the tire mate solidly. When everything is lined up, inflate the tire to its full pressure, and replace the wheel in the bike. If you used rim tape, it's generally okay to ride the bike immediately. If you used glue you should wait about 12 hours to let the adhesive set. But if you must ride, it's generally all right provided you take it easy around corners.

ADJUSTING WHEEL HUBS

When your wheels start wiggling side to side because the hubs are too loose or stop spinning smoothly because they're too tight, it's time for a little hub adjustment. What this amounts to is tightening or loosening a special nut called a *cone*. (See exploded view of hub.) When looking at a fully assembled hub, the cone will look just like another nut, but with two grooves on either side, which are meant to receive the edges of a hub spanner, a special wrenchlike tool available in most bike stores. (You'll usually need two of them.) The cone is so called because it has a cone-shaped segment that extends inside the hub, where it presses against the ball bearings. If screwed in too far, the bearings will not have enough play and the axle will bind. If not far enough, the wheel will wiggle sloppily. Adjustment is simply

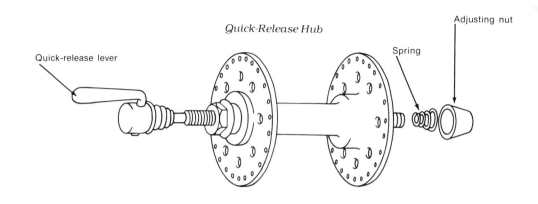

Quick-Release Hub

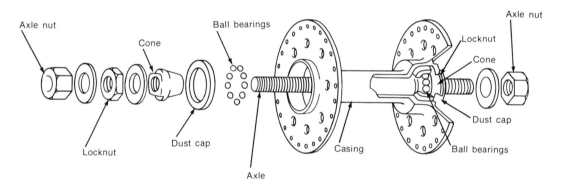

Standard Hub

a matter of turning the cone in and out with the spanner until you get the kind of wheel action you like.

There are two sets of instructions: one for standard hubs, and one for quick-release models. You'll need a couple of spanners, a wrench, and perhaps a vise for quick-release hubs.

Standard Hubs

There is one definite advantage standard hubs have over quick-release hubs—adjustment can be made with the wheels left on the bike. Look at the left side of the hub. On the oustide you should find an axle nut or a wingnut. Right next to this will be the fork blade, then a washer, a locknut, another washer, and then the cone. Beyond that, you'll see a dust cap and inside will be bearings and lubricant, but leave this latter assembly alone.

Now, your bike may be different than just described because some manufacturers skip one or even both of the washers, and some bikes have no locknut. In this case, the axle nut serves as the locknut and the fork blade pulls double duty as the washer.

You really only need to work on the left side of the hub because the right-side assembly can act as an anchor while you tighten or loosen the left cone. In fact, many right-side cones don't even have slots in them for a spanner to grip. Here's what to do:

1. Loosen the axle nut or wingnut on the left.

2. Loosen the locknut slightly, with a spanner.

3. Now tighten the cone against the bearings, then loosen it slightly. (If you can't tighten the cone, perhaps the problem was that it must be loosened.)

4. Tighten the locknut back against the cone.

5. Test the wheel. If it still wiggles, you have to repeat the process. If the wheel won't spin well, you've over-tightened the cone. Loosen the lock-nut off the cone, and then loosen the cone off the bearings and retighten the locknut. Retest. Basically, this is a trial-and-error affair, involving tightening and loosening and retightening. When tightening the locknut, be care-ful that you aren't tightening the cone also. And though you can do this with one spanner, it's handy to have two so that you can hold the cone steady with one spanner as you tighten the lock-nut with the other.

6. When you're satisfied with the wheel's action, tighten the axle nut, and you're finished.

If you can't get the wheel to spin freely without wiggling, no matter how hard you try, the hub probably needs overhauling. We suggest you take it to a bike shop for this.

Quick-Release Hubs

You must remove the wheel from the bike if you have quick-release hubs, and you will definitely need two span-ners. You will also need a vise.

1. Remove the quick-release unit from the hub. Unscrew the adjusting nut (see illustration on page 112). Then, holding onto the lever, pull the skewer through the middle of the hub. You should hold the lever and skewer in one hand while adjusting the nut with the other. Screw the nut loosely back on the shaft so that you don't lose the springs in the unit. Now you're ready to work on the hub itself.

2. Clamp the wheel in a soft-jawed vise, if possible. If not, find a strong friend to hold it while you work on it. To adjust the hub, follow the same directions given for standard wheels, but with one exception. Unlike a stan-dard hub, which has a tight right axle nut to keep the right-side assembly intact, the quick-release hub now has both sides free to move. This means you'll have to work on both sides at the same time, which is why you'll need two spanners. Keep one on the right-side locknut to keep it station-ary while you adjust the left-side lock-nut and cone. Adjust both cones to get the best results. Again, if the wheel cannot be adjusted into condition, the hub probably needs an overhaul, which is best done by a professional.

3. Slip the quick-release shaft back in the axle, and replace the adjusting nut on the other side before putting the wheel back on the bike.

FIXING CHAIN PROBLEMS

The chain is often the most forgotten part of the bike. People ignore it for years and then seem amazed they have trouble with it. With nothing more elaborate than an old rag, a small can of oil, and a minute of your time, you can keep your chain flowing smoothly over your sprockets. Here are the most common problems you are likely to run up against.

Squeaky Chain

A chain is made up of hundreds of small moving parts. Each link is con-nected to the next by a small rivet, and every other link is made up of a small pair of rollers that help make the movement of the chain over the teeth of the sprocket smooth and even. What happens when all these parts are ignored is that they dry out and dirt from the road works its way inside. As a result, you have to pedal harder to get up speed and your chain starts squeaking in agony.

Before you put a drop of oil on your chain, examine the links. Most likely you'll see dirt and grit jammed between the links if you've never done anything to the chain before. Wipe off the chain with your rag to get rid of some of this. You can poke free the larger clumps of dirt with the blade of a screwdriver. If the chain still seems a little dirty, you could put a little kerosene or turpentine on the rag and wipe off the chain. This should help. If you want to get it even cleaner, you can remove it and soak it in either of these fluids. (That's more complicated and is covered later in "Removing a Chain," a section to follow.)

Once the chain is clean, get out your can of oil. For oiling the chain on a 3-speed or a 10-speed bike, simply hold the can pointed down over one spot and backpedal the chain underneath it, squeezing out a small trickle of oil over the links as they move underneath. Don't be too generous with the oil. Just let enough trickle down to dampen each link as it passes by. If you have a bike with a coaster brake, you'll have to turn the bike upside down and rotate the pedals forward, the way you would ordinarily pedal, and then trickle the oil onto the moving chain.

Once you've covered the whole chain with oil this way, take your rag and start wiping off the excess oil. A chain that is slick with too much oil will attract dirt and grit and give some of the same problems you had before.

Skipping Chain

Every so often, your chain will skip off your front or rear gears. This is nothing to worry about unless it seems to happen nearly every time you ride your bike. The cure is simple for 1- and 3-speed bikes. Simply loosen your axle nuts, and pull your rear wheel back farther, until the chain is a little more taut. Center the wheel, and tighten the axle in place.

On a 10-speed bike, the answer is not quite as simple. Your rear gear changer has a spring that is supposed to automatically keep your chain taut. If your chain does not seem taut, it could be either because there is something wrong with that spring or because your chain has stretched. You can tell if a chain on any bike—from 1-speeds to 10-speeds—is stretched by two simple tests. First, stand so that you are looking down at the chain. Now gently pull it out to the right. If you can pull it more than an inch or centimeter out from its natural alignment, you probably have a stretched chain. Second, grab a length of the chain with your hands about 6 inches (15 centimeters) apart. First move your hands toward each other and then pull them apart. If you feel a hesitation and a give, your chain has stretched. Either way, if your chain has stretched you should consider replacing it. You can have a bike mechanic do this or, you can do it yourself.

Removing a Chain

There are several advantages to knowing how to remove your bicycle chain. You can get it thoroughly clean by removing it and giving it a good soak in kerosene or turpentine. You can make adjustments in it such as shortening a slightly stretched chain and using it again. The next sections explain how to remove a chain on 3- and 10-speeds.

1- and 3-Speed Bikes. Getting a chain off a 1-speed or 3-speed bike is the simpler challenge of the two you are likely to face if you decide to try removing a chain. The reason is that the chains on these bikes have a weak link, better known as a *master link*, that is made to be taken apart. If you have these kinds of bikes, slowly move the chain in front of you and before long you will see one link that is slightly different from the others. This is the master link.

There are two types of master links. One is an elongated U-shaped clip holding one link together; the other, a slightly larger oval plate hooked over the tips of two rivets. To take off either of these, all you need is a narrow-tipped screwdriver.

To open the U-shaped master link, get the blade of the screwdriver in between the legs of the U and spread them apart. If may take a little wiggling but the U should gradually work free. Then you can separate the chain at this point and, for example, soak the chain well in a kerosene bath to clean it up.

The oval plate can be pried off the rivet tips with that same screwdriver and, once it's free, the chain should come apart easily. Finally, when you reassemble chains with either type of master link, make sure you replace the chain so that the open side of the master link is facing out. This makes it easier to reattach the chain and, more importantly, will make it easier to remove the master link should you ever have to do it again. The U-shaped clip will slip back into place over the rivet tips while the oval master link might be a little problem. Use a pair of pliers if you have to so that you can squeeze the rivet tips more closely together and slip the oval plate back over them.

10-Speed Bikes. Before you can do anything to the chain on a 10-speed bike, you will have to add a rather special item to your tool kit. It's an odd little device called the chain link removal tool, or chain tool for short. It's available in most bike shops and is not very expensive.

There are slight variations in what this kind of tool looks like, but generally it resembles a miniature vise on a stick. The screw that you turn has a T-handle at one end and a steel nub or finger at the other. Perpendicular to where the steel finger pokes through, run two notched metal ridges parallel with each other. The chain link fits over one or another of these ridges, depending on what you want to do.

To use this gadget, set a chain link onto one of the notched ridges, which automatically lines up the rivet with the steel finger at the end of the T-screw. As you turn the screw, the steel finger pushes the rivet out of (or back into) the chain link.

Let's suppose you want to remove a chain link. The first thing to do is set the link on the notched ridge farther

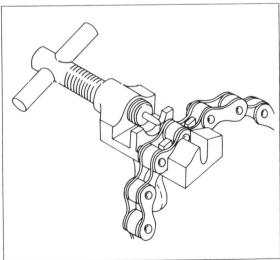

The chain-link removal tool is about as specialized a tool as you will need, but its use is simple to learn.

away from where that steel finger pokes through. Now slowly turn the T-handle clockwise until you push the rivet almost all the way, but not quite, out. Push the rivet just far enough so that it frees the link but not so far that it gets pushed completely out of the chain link.

Take the chain off the tool, and try to wiggle the chain apart. If it doesn't come free right away, hold the chain with the side where the rivet is poking through away from you and bend the chain outward just a little. Now it should separate with ease. If you decide that your chain needs replacing, take it to a bike shop and make sure to get a chain exactly like it. Chains do vary slightly in their specifications, and you'll want one that meshes well with the teeth on your sprockets. Very often the new chain you buy will be longer than you need. Measure it against your old chain and completely remove the rivet in the link to break the chain where you want. Before you do this, make sure that it has a wide "female" link on one end and a narrow "male" link on the other so that the chain will go back together.

Suppose, for example, you just wanted to clean your chain and now want to put it back on the bike. First, run the chain through the small wheel in your rear derailleur, or gear changer, and position it so that it is loosely draped around your front crank. Make sure the side of the chain with the rivet poking out is on the outside of the bike. This will make it easier to work with.

Now take the two ends of the chain and poke half the narrow link inside half the wide link, making sure the holes in the links line up. Put this partly reassembled link in your chain tool on the ridge closer to where that skinny steel finger pokes through.

Again, slowly rotate the T-handle clockwise, making sure the fingertip lines up with the tip of the rivet, which should be sticking out on the side of the chain toward the handle. If your chain holes are correctly aligned, the steel finger should easily push the rivet back into the hole. Be extremely careful as you get to the end of the push. The rivet should be seated in the hole so that it protrudes an equal amount from either side. If it sticks out too far on one side, it could jam in the rear gears or gear changer. Back-pedal the chain slowly to make sure that this doesn't happen. If it does seem to catch, put the chain link back on the tool and poke the offending side in more deeply.

FIXING 3-SPEED SHIFTERS

Because it's almost fully encased in your rear hub, a 3-speed shift mechanism is relatively trouble-free—at least compared to a 10-speed derailleur system. And when there is trouble, the gears can be set right again with just a screwdriver and some oil. Two common problems are described in the following sections.

Slipping Gears

When you suddenly feel no resistance while pedaling, then you have slipping gears. Your feet spin wildly but the bike goes nowhere. The first thing to check is the actual shift-lever mechanism. It may be that the whole assembly is slipping around and needs tightening.

If that's not the problem, look at the small valve, usually plastic, with a cap on it on the rear hub. Flick it open with your fingernail or screwdriver and squirt in three or four drops of oil. Close the valve, and spin the wheel to work the oil into the shift mechanism. If this does not solve the problem,

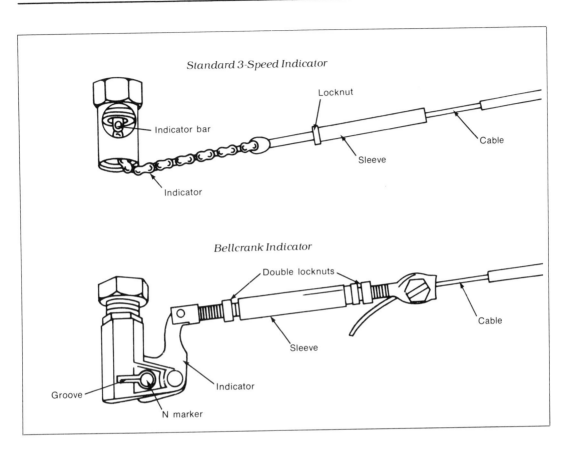

Standard 3-Speed Indicator

Locknut

Indicator bar

Cable

Sleeve

Indicator

Bellcrank Indicator

Double locknuts

Cable

Sleeve

Groove

Indicator

N marker

don't attempt to open the hub. The workings of a 3-speed shifter are a nightmare to a novice or professional mechanic. Take the bike to a good repair shop.

No Low Gear

When a hub shifter goes out of adjustment, one of the first symptoms is an inability to shift it into first gear. You adjust a 3-speed shifter by adjusting the *indicator*. This is the part that connects the shift cable to the hub. Most of you will have a standard mechanism (see illustration above). Some will have a bellcrank indicator (see illustration above).

To adjust bikes with a standard indicator, shift the bike into second gear, sometimes labeled "N" for normal. Now go to the rear of the bike and

look through the hole in the nut that comes out of the axle. You should see a small chain connected to a small steel bar. This is the indicator bar. The tip of the bar, connected to the last link in the chain, should be visible through the hole. If it isn't—and if the shifter is out of adjustment, it probably won't be—you'll have to turn the adjustor sleeve. This is the sleeve that is connected to the small chain (see illustration shown above). In front of it is a locknut. Loosen this, and turn the sleeve until you have the indicator bar lined up in the hole. Now tighten back the locknut and you're set.

For those of you with bellcrank indicators, adjust this type of shifter very much the same way as the standard indicator. Put the bike in second gear, or N. But instead of looking

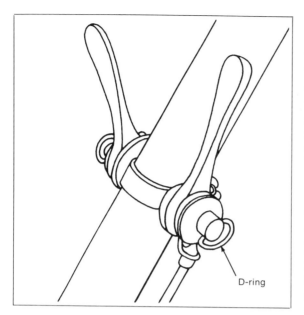

D-ring

When your D-ring needs tightening, your derailleur will keep slipping you up to your highest gear—an uncomfortable and surprising phenomenon that is easily avoided.

through a hole in the axle nut, you'll find a nut with an N on it and a groove next to it. You'll also find a sleeve that's held by two locknuts instead of one. Loosen both locknuts and turn the sleeve until the N and the groove are lined up. Then retighten the locknuts. If this doesn't solve your shifting problems, see a mechanic.

FIXING 10-SPEED SHIFTERS

Ten-speed shifters, or derailleurs, are vulnerable to all sorts of problems. Fortunately, most of them can be corrected with just a screwdriver and some oil. There are two derailleurs— one in front and one in the rear, which will be discussed separately. First, there are a couple of things that can foul up your shifting that really have nothing to do with the derailleurs.

A common phenomenon is unwanted "automatic" shifting. Your derailleur keeps putting you into the highest gear without you even touching the shift lever. As dramatic as this may seem, it's easily remedied. What's happening is that the levers are loose. The derailleurs are spring loaded, and if the lever isn't holding onto the cable hard enough, the derailleurs (the rear especially) will automatically push the chain onto the smallest gear. Look at the sides of your shift levers. All you need do is tighten the little D-ring on the side (see illustration on this page). Or perhaps your model has a wingnut or, on cheaper models, a screwhead.

The opposite can also happen. Shifting becomes extremely difficult. Then your levers are simply too tight. However, just loosening the D-rings or wingnuts on the levers will probably not solve this problem. Levers don't normally tighten by themselves. In most cases, it means the insides of the mechanism are full of dirt and grit.

You'll have to unscrew the D-ring all the way, take the lever apart, clean all the parts, and put everything back together. There are a lot of parts involved, so lay each part out in a line as you take it off so that you can remember the proper order to replace them.

If the levers are operating smoothly, then your problems must be solved through either rear or front derailleur adjustment.

Rear Derailleur

The rear derailleur does the bulk of the work and is likely to be the source of most of your troubles. Adjustment problems can be reduced to these four main possibilities:

• The derailleur won't throw the chain into high gear (the smallest, outermost rear sprocket).
• The derailleur throws the chain past high gear totally off the sprocket and onto the chain stays.
• The derailleur won't put the chain into low gear (the biggest, innermost rear sprocket).
• The derailleur throws the chain past low gear and in against the wheel or spoke protector.

Adjusting the derailleur so that it doesn't do these things is often turned into a mysterious process. And while it sometimes requires a hideous amount of trial-and-error to get it to work right, the underlying principles are relatively simple.

Adjusting the gears is done by two screws. One screw controls the outward movement of the chain toward the higher (smaller in size) gears. The other controls inward throw toward the lower (bigger in size) gears. All these screws really do is physically prevent the derailleur from moving in one direction or the other. When the derailleur hits the end of each screw in either direction, bang, it stops. So by loosening a screw, you allow the

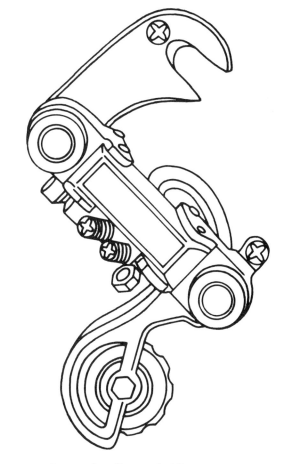

Adjusting the rear derailleur so that it performs just right can be a time-consuming process, but it's not beyond the capability of a careful and patient cyclist.

derailleur to travel farther; by tightening, you limit it. On most derailleurs, the low-gear screw is the top one. And on many models, the screws are labeled with L and H for low and high. But if there is no labeling, you can easily find out which is which by experimenting.

Before you start adjusting, though, you'll have to get the bike off the ground so that you can turn the pedals and shift the bike. It is also best to adjust the rear derailleur with the chain kept on the small (inside) front chainwheel. Then you're ready to work on the four main problems mentioned above.

1. Derailleur throws chain off the small sprocket: With the chain back on the gear, tighten the high-gear screw a quarter revolution at a time (usually clockwise) until the shifter stops throwing off the chain as you turn the pedals.

2. Derailleur won't shift chain into high gear: Simply reverse the above procedure. Loosen high-gear screw a quarter-turn at a time until you can shift onto smallest sprocket, but without throwing the chain off.

3. Shifter throws chain past largest sprocket and in toward the wheel: Procedure is the same as for Number 1, except that the low-gear screw is tightened.

4. Derailleur won't shift into low gear: Follow instructions for Number 2, but use low-gear screw. However, sometimes this problem is caused by a stretched derailleur cable. Have your bike store replace it if this is the case.

Front Derailleur

Adjustment for the front derailleur is pretty straightforward, though sometimes it can be a bit more delicate, so it is best to restrict yourself to turning the adjustment screws in very small increments. Normally, the inside screw is for inside throw; the outside screw, for outside throw. The procedure is basically the same as for rear derailleur adjustment. The only extra thing to remember is this: When adjusting for outward throw, shift the chain to

Simple front derailleurs are the pole type, below, which have one adjusting screw facing outwards. Nearly all other mechanisms are parallelogram types, below, which have two adjusting screws on top: for low gears (inside) and for high gears (outside).

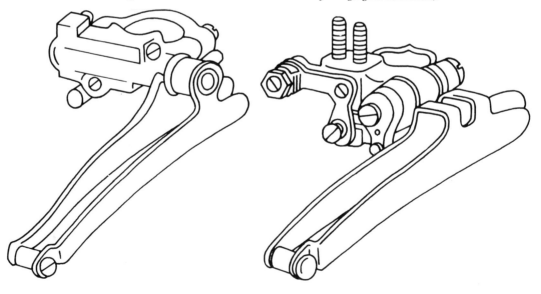

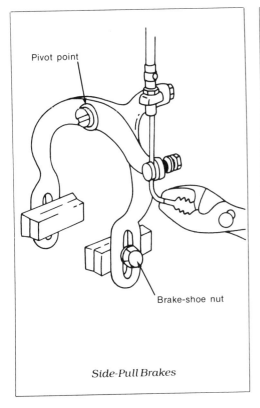

Side-Pull Brakes

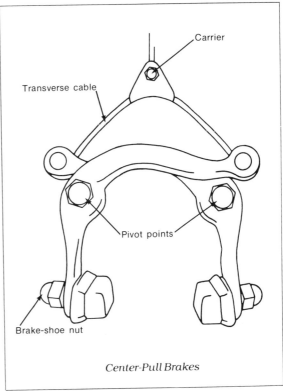

Center-Pull Brakes

the smallest sprocket in back; when adjusting for inward throw, put the chain on the largest gear.

FIXING BRAKE PROBLEMS

Bicycle brakes appear simple, but they're sometimes difficult to work on—difficult to diagnose what's wrong with them and awkward to fix. For most repairs you will need a crescent wrench, pliers, possibly a vise-grip and some oil. As mentioned in Chapter 1 there are two kinds of brakes: side-pulls and center-pulls (both types are illustrated above). Both are repaired in similar ways.

Sticky Brakes

Brake action is slow with sticky brakes. And brakes are especially slow in returning to their open position after you have released the levers. This probably means that the brake cable is sticking inside its housing. Try to put a drop of oil in each end of the housing. Now click the brake lever open and shut rapidly several times. This should spread the oil through the housing. But if it doesn't go to the bike store and get new cables and housings, preferably the Teflon-coated kind—they are a pleasure to use and never need lubricating.

Centering Problems

When the brake is open, each brake shoe should be the same distance from the rim to be centered correctly. If they're not, try loosening the bolt that holds the brake to the frame (use a crescent wrench, not pliers). Re-center the brake and retighten the bolt. In many cases, however, this doesn't solve the problem.

If it doesn't, try oiling the pivot points. On a side-pull brake, there is only one pivot point, and this is the whole assembly held together by the big centering bolt. On center-pulls, the pivot points are two bolts that the arms swing around on.

You can also try tapping the brake spring on side-pulls with a hammer and pin or by loosening the mounting bolt very slightly. Don't expect to get your brakes perfectly centered, however, unless you have an expensive pair of Campagnolo side-pulls, or some equivalent.

Weak Brakes

You should only have to squeeze your brake levers shut about 2 inches (5 centimeters) or less before the brake pads hit the rim and start to stop you. If you find yourself squeezing the levers almost to the handlebars in order to stop the bike, you have weak brakes, and it's time for some repairs. This problem is usually caused by one of two things: a stretched cable or badly worn brake pads.

Stretched Cable. If the brake pads aren't worn, then the cable has stretched. It's now too long, and you have to shorten it. First, check to see if you have adjustable brakes. If the cable is attached to the brake arms with a disc-and-screw assembly instead of a nut, just tighten the disc to shorten the cable. If not, you'll have to pull the slack out with a pliers. Here's where a friend or a piece of string comes in useful. Have your friend hold the brake arms on the wheel so that the pads are tight against the rim while you loosen the nut that holds the cable and pull the slack out with your pliers. (See illustration on page 121.) And if you don't have a friend, use the string instead to hold the

brake closed. When you've got the cable taut again, tighten the nut.

Be forewarned that tightening that nut may not be an easy affair. On side-pulls it's fairly straightforward. But center-pulls are another story because the cable is not connected directly to the brake arms. Instead, the cable is attached to the *carrier*, which is a triangular-shaped sleeve above the brake arms that's connected to them by a separate transverse cable (see illustration on page 121). The cable nut is on the carrier, so to adjust the brakes you must hold the carrier up while you pull down on the cable and tighten the nut at the same time. Ideally, you should get a friend to hold up the carrier while you pull out the slack with your pliers and tighten the nut with your other hand. Otherwise, use a small socket wrench. With this kind of tool you can tighten the nut and hold up the carrier in one motion while your hand is free to work the pliers.

Worn Pads. Brake pads wear out eventually. But they're cheap, so don't delay in replacing them. It's also an easy job.

With some brake-shoe assemblies, all you have to replace are the rubber pads themselves. Simply slip the old ones out by pushing them backwards out of the grooves in the shoes. Then push in the new pads.

If you must buy a whole new shoe assembly, take a look at the illustration on page 121. Note that there's a slot in the brake arms that allows a variety of heights and angles for the shoes. The best way to position the new shoes is to take out the old ones using your wrench, and note the marks left by the old brake shoe nuts. Just lock in the new shoes in the same position—at least to begin with. Then check to see if the pads hit the rim; no part of the pad should contact the tire itself. The pads should also be within ⅛ inch (3 millimeters) of the rim when the brakes are not being applied. Some brake shoes are designed so that they *toe in*, that is, the front of the pads are slightly closer to the wheel than the backs. This is fine. It's also fine if the pads are equidistant from the rim along their entire lengths. But the rear of a pad should never be closer than the leading edge. If so, try re-shaping the brake arms carefully, using your vise-grip.

When you get back on the bike and apply the brakes, new brake pads will often squeak. In time, they wear in and stop making that noise.

FIXING PEDAL PROBLEMS

With your adjustable crescent wrench and a can of oil you can take care of most of the problems you'll have with your pedals. Probably the most common problems are sticky and loose pedals.

Sticky Pedals

When you hit your pedals lightly, they should spin freely. If they don't move at all or barely spin around, they probably need some lubrication. Put a few drops of oil at the end near where the pedal is screwed into the crank, and spin it to work the oil in. Some of the better rat-trap style pedals also have a removable dust cap on the outside of the pedal (see illustration at right). Some pry off, some screw off. You'll have to examine yours to see which kind they are.

If you have the type of pedals with dust caps, remove the dust cap and squirt in a few drops of oil. (Most likely you'll be able to see the ball bearings in there that need the lubrication.) Spin the pedal to work in the oil, and replace the dust cap.

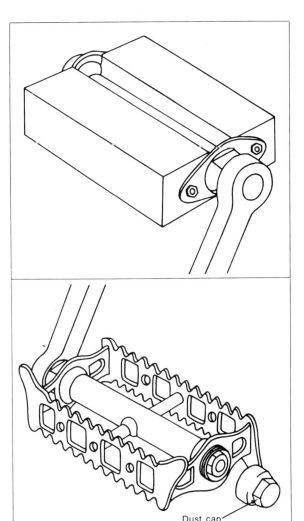

Dust cap

The most common problems you'll have with both a rubber pedal (top) and a rat-trap pedal (bottom) are stickiness and looseness.

Loose Pedals

Every so often you may notice that one or even both of your pedals seem to jiggle as you ride. Most likely the problem is that they have worked themselves loose from the cranks and need to be screwed in again. Usually you can do this with your crescent wrench.

Each pedal tightens in opposite directions. To tighten the right pedal into the crank, turn it clockwise. To tighten the left pedal, turn it counterclockwise. Never let a pedal work itself loose. You run the risk of damaging the threads on the pedal or on the cranks or on both. If your attempts to tighten it don't work, take your bike to a mechanic. You may have stripped the threads on the pedal or in the crank.

FIXING CRANK PROBLEMS

Your crank arms are relatively maintenance free. But sometimes they work loose and must be tightened. If you get in an accident and one gets bent or broken, you should take your bike to a store for repairs. But you can take care of tightening cranks yourself. As explained in Chapter 1, there are three kinds of cranks: one-piece, cottered, and cotterless.

One-Piece

This very simple kind of crank will not come loose from the bottom bracket spindle that connects it to the crank on the other side for a very simple reason: both cranks and the spindle are one continuous piece. This is a rather trouble-free way of designing cranks, but if any part of the assembly breaks, you have to take it to a bike shop and replace the whole unit.

Cottered

These are the most common kind of cranks and are so-called because each crank is held to the spindle via a cotter pin that goes through the crank, the spindle, and is secured on the other side by a cotter-pin nut. You can feel when the crank is loose by the sloppiness and jerkiness it will give your pedaling motion. If so, tighten the crank as quickly as possible because a slipping crank can wear both itself and the spindle out of shape.

Begin by tightening the crank by tightening the cotter-pin nut. If this doesn't work, and it may not, either tap the cotter pin tighter or replace the entire pin should it be bent or broken. If you feel at all hesitant in your ability to do this, take the bike to a shop that has special tools for tapping in or tapping out cotter pins.

If you want to try fixing the pin yourself, get a light hammer and wooden block. Remove the cotter-pin nut, and place the wooden block beneath that end of the pin. Make sure the crank is resting firmly on the block, and then tap in the cotter pin by hitting it very lightly on its head with the hammer. Banging it too hard will ruin the bearings in the bottom bracket. When finished, replace the cotter-pin nut.

Should the pin be bent or broken, replace it using the same method.

Cotterless

To tighten cotterless cranks, you'll need a special cotterless tool. Make sure to get the same brand tool as your cranks as most of these tools are not compatible with different brands. Tightening is important because cotterless cranks are made of light, strong, but soft, aluminum alloy. And this means that their axle holes can be reamed out of shape if the cranks are loose. New cranks take a while before they set up tight; so if you've got a new bike, it doesn't hurt to tighten the cranks every 25 miles (40 kilometers) or so for the first 100 miles (160 kilometers). After that, it's just a matter of when they feel loose, which you'll be able to detect fairly easily.

On most models, you'il have to remove a protective dust cap before getting to the cotterless bolt. If the dust cap has a long slit in it, you can remove it with a large screwdriver, those with a hexagonal opening require a 5 mm Allen wrench. After the cap is off, you'll find a large bolt inside. Put the crank socket tool on the bolt and tighten it hard. To see if it's tight enough, hold the opposite crank steady in one hand and try to move the crank you just tightened with the other. If it gives, even a little, then it's not tight enough. If it won't tighten up, it's possible the axle opening has already been distorted and you'll have to get a new crank.

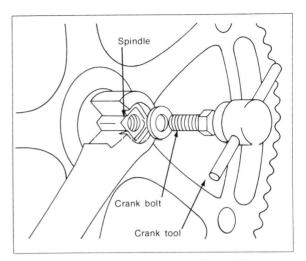

To tighten a cotterless crank, you need a crank tool. Make sure you get the right socket and extractor for your brand of cranks. Cotterless sets are generally made of soft alloy and must be handled carefully.

Chapter 8

EQUIPMENT: THE BEST AND THE BEST BUYS

The recommendations here are based on our experiences with different bicycle components, on the considered opinion of other experienced bicyclists, and on our own personal prejudices about what good equipment is. Show this book to another bike expert, and you may get some different recommendations based on that person's biases. We won't pretend that this is the last word in your guide to bicycle components, but if you take up any of our suggestions, you won't be disappointed.

Although it might seem that way, our "best by far" components were not chosen for their high price but for their fine workmanship and durability. Some of them are lifetime investments. Our "good buys" are chosen mostly for their durability and price. They may not be as finely crafted as some of their more expensive counter-parts and they may even look a little crude by comparison, but they do what they're supposed to do and do it well at a fraction of the cost.

Finally there were a few areas, such as with bicycle pumps and helmets, where we felt there were no "bargain" items. Cheap bicycle pumps tend to be just that, cheap in every way. For a reasonable amount of money, you can buy a decent pump that will last for years. (We can and have spent more on trying out and throwing away cheaper models.) And since the right bicycle helmet can be literally a life or death purchase, we only recommend buying the best you can afford. Cheap helmets offer little or no protection and, we feel, do not even deserve mentioning. As for the other equipment items mentioned in this chapter, let your personal preference and your pocket-book be your guide.

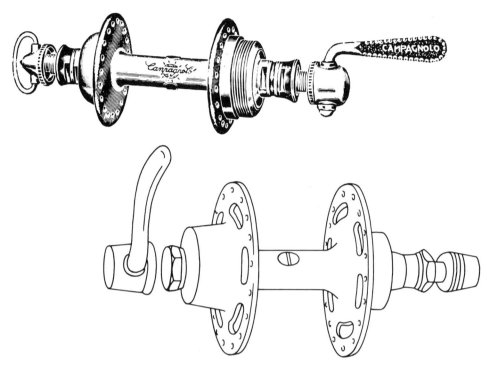

Campagnolo Record hubs (top) are durable and dependable—and, of course, expensive. Shimano hubs (bottom) are a cheaper, but adequate, substitute.

HUBS

Best by Far: Campagnolo Nuovo Record hubs are the slickest spinning hubs on the market today. Many other manufacturers have come out with sealed-bearing hubs—a very good idea —while Campagnolo has remained content to continue with their traditional models that require periodic adjustment and regular overhauls. Still, most cyclists agree that they're worth it. Campagnolo hubs are expensive, but many of the new, sealed and titanium hubs have caught up with, and in some cases surpassed, them in price. But not in quality.

A Good Buy: The best hubs seem to come from Europe or California these days. But they're all expensive, too. So we reluctantly recommend the Japanese Shimano alloy hubs as a cash-saving alternative. They're about half the price of the Nuovo Record, have quick-release levers, and will do the job for most cycle tourists.

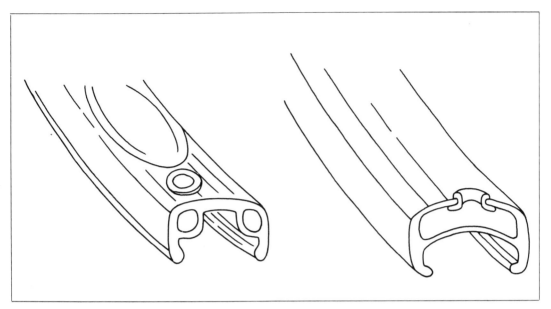

Super Champion Alloy clincher rims (left) are strong, durable, and very popular, especially for long-distance touring. The Mavic Type 3

clincher rim (right) is 22 mm wide, which means it can take any standard or high-pressure clincher tire.

CLINCHER (HIGH-PRESSURE) RIMS

Best by Far: This is a difficult area. We'll say Super Champion alloy clincher rims are the best—but not with utter confidence. Many cyclists prefer the Mavic Elan or the Weinmann concave-style rims. The Super Champions may be slightly heavier than these others, but they have a good reputation for strength. And also—like the Mavics and Weinmanns —they are made to be compatible with the new high-pressure low-profile clincher tires.

A Good Buy: The Mavic Type 3 rim is really not much less expensive than the Super Champion. But it could save you trouble and money because it is compatible with a wide range of tires—standard or high-pressure.

CLINCHER (HIGH-PRESSURE) TIRES

Because they're made of thicker rubber and have heavier treads, clincher tires are sometimes considered ideal for touring, especially on rough roads. But because they have usually been inflated to lower pressures than sew-up tires, they are considered to give a softer ride and one that is slower as well because more of the tire touches the road. So the choices you have are: if you want a sturdy tire that gives you a minimum of flats, get a clincher tire; if you want a "fast" tire and are willing to put up with your share of flat tires, get sew-up tires and rims. But, as explained in the following sections, now these distinctions between the two types don't always apply.

Best by Far: Tire making has recently become a little more sophisticated. There are now clincher tires that can be pumped up to the high pressures of sew-ups, giving you that hard responsive ride while at the same time offering you some of the toughness of the clincher. You have a broad and baffling choice of these high-pressure clinchers, but if money is no object, we feel you should get the brand known as the Specialized Touring Tire. The center of the tire is a heavy rubber ridge that gives you minimal, low-friction contact with the road, and the sides of the tire surface have a herringbone tread to help grip the road when you corner. It comes in two sizes—27 x 1¼/700X 32C and 27 x 1⅛/700X 28C. Many people prefer the 27 x 1¼/700X 32C size since they claim they get fewer flats with the

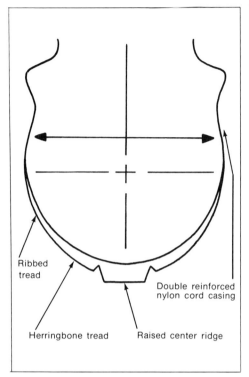

The Specialized Touring Tire is resilient, lightweight, and yet strong enough to withstand long rides at high pressure. It reduces rolling friction, extends tread life, and offers excellent traction for braking and cornering.

wider size. The Specialized Touring Tire can be inflated up to 95 pounds (42 kilograms), putting it in the same league as some sew-ups.

A Good Buy: If a hard, fast ride is not all that important to you and you don't feel like spending the extra money for such a specialized tire, a good alternative is the model known as the IRC High Pressure Tire. This will take up to 85 pounds (38 kilograms) of pressure and for less money will give you a decent ride.

SEW-UP TIRES

Best by Far: Our favorite by far is the Clement Campionato del Mondo. This is a beautiful silk touring tire that's also commonly used by racers as a training tire because it's so tough and flat-resistant. It has a fairly wide profile and is reasonably heavy, about 290 grams. Some riders criticize del Mondos for their profile and weight, saying you might as well switch to a clincher tire. We don't think so. They're still a good 50 grams lighter than today's lightest high-pressure clinchers, and they'll take a bit more pressure (a maximum of about 115 psi). Also silk tires have a very special, responsive feel that a clincher cannot imitate. Another good silk tire is the Clement Criterium. It's lighter, at 250 grams, and more suited to racing, though some tourists ride on it. Both the del Mondo and the Criterium are expensive.

A Good Buy: Here, we reluctantly recommend the Clement Elvezia. It's less than half the price of the del Mondo. It's made of cotton, and it's heavier, about 350 grams. If you have to skimp on sew-up tires, it might be better to think about changing to high-pressure clinchers, which are about the same weight, less prone to flats, and much easier to repair. Not to mention the fact that they're less than half the price of even the Elvezia. Still, if what you've got are sew-up wheels and you need a good, reasonably priced tire, the Elvezia will do you fine.

SEW-UP RIMS

Best by Far: For sew-up rims, we also select Super Champion, but again not to the exclusion of all others. Many riders swear by Fiamme sew-up rims; others by Mavic. It all has to do with your own personal experience with various brands. Whether a rim holds up or not has a lot to do with the workmanship involved in putting the wheel together—but in most cases the rim will get either the credit or the blame or the wheel's sturdiness, or lack of it. Super Champions come in several different weights, and unless you plan to ride only on smooth roads, we recommend the heavier model.

A Good Buy: None, really. All sew-up rims are pretty expensive, so it comes down to a matter of taste, weight, and where you plan to ride. If you find a really cheap, heavy sew-up rim, we recommend you not buy it. What's the point? Clincher rims and tires are getting so light and so fast that it no longer makes sense to buy cheap sew-up wheels. Switch to clinchers instead.

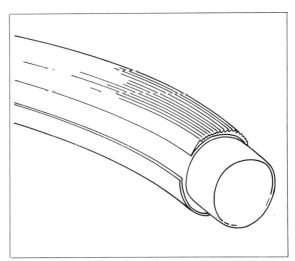

The Clement Campionato del Mondo is a wide-profile silk tire that is held in generally high esteem both among racers and touring cyclists.

HANDLEBARS AND STEMS

It's difficult to talk about these two components separately because among the better brands, the handlebars and stems are so finely tooled that they only fit each other. For that reason, they are discussed together.

The Cinelli Road Stem 1/Record has a hidden binder bolt (see cut away illustration at right) that is easily tightened by an interior wedge. The design limits the smallest size to 10 cm.

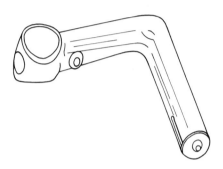
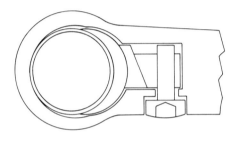

Handlebars

Professional cyclists look for two qualities in handlebars. One is durability. Riders can take some spectacular spills in the course of a tough road race and their bikes suffer tremendous punishment as a result. The last thing they want is a set of handlebars that get bent out of shape in a fall. The second quality they seek is lightness. The less a component like handlebars weighs, the less work they have to do to keep up their speed. Shaving off a few grams here and there all contributes, in the end, to a much lighter-weight bike.

Best by Far: If you have professional tastes and the budget to match, invest in a set of Cinelli handlebars. These hard-to-get Italian components are almost universally regarded as the best there is.

A Good Buy: An excellent budget choice is a set of SR (for Sakae Ringyo) handlebars, which sell for about half the cost of a set of Cinellis.

Stems

Once you've committed yourself to a particular brand of handlebars, at least in these two instances, you will have to invest in handlebar stems made by the same companies. They are specifically sized for those companies' handlebars, so don't let a salesperson who may not have them in stock tell you otherwise. Cinelli bars fit only Cinelli stems and SR bars are destined for SR stems.

Best by Far: The best model of Cinelli stems now out is the Cinelli Road Stem 1/Record. It's an extremely light and beautifully tooled component that lets you adjust the angle or height of your handlebars with a few effortless turns of its unique, hidden binder bolt. Make sure you get an Allen Key— an L-shaped hexagonal bar—to fit this stem bolt.

A Good Buy: For your SR handlebar, get a Super Light SR stem if you're worried about weight. These are made of duraluminum.

FRAME MATERIAL

There are all sorts of exotic frame materials these days: graphite, aluminum, titanium. But we'd recommend sticking with steel.

Best by Far: The best steel tubing is Reynolds 531 double butted. It's the choice of many racers and also makes for a good touring bike. Just as good is Columbus tubing. Some racers prefer Columbus because it's heavier and stiffer than Reynolds 531. But that may make it too harsh for many recreational cyclists.

A Good Buy: Ishiwata is a decent, more reasonably priced brand of tubing. It can cut $40 or $50 (£18 or £22) off the price of a frame. But some cyclists complain that it's not stiff enough for a vigorous rider.

BRAKES

Best by Far: Campagnolo makes the best set of brakes. They are side-pulls, and they are works of art. The smooth quick-release device on the brakes is widely copied, so is the adjusting mechanism, which allows you to tighten the cable to get rid of the slack that comes with age and stretching. Campagnolo brakes also have a special centering nut that allows you to center each brake when necessary. Trying to center a side-pull brake can be a frustrating experience, and Campagnolo's remedy to this problem is a good one. At this writing, there are many, many copies of the Campagnolo side-pull—all of them are cheaper, but none of them are quite as good.

A Good Buy: A much cheaper side-pull is the venerable Universal 68. It's about 30 percent of the cost of a Campagnolo. It's been used by cyclists for several years and has stood up to the test of time. But it's not nearly as pretty as the Campagnolo brakes nor does it have the convenience features, but it will stop your bike if you keep it in good repair.

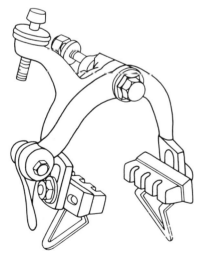

Campagnolo is the best there is—and their brakes not only function beautifully but are beautiful to look at as well.

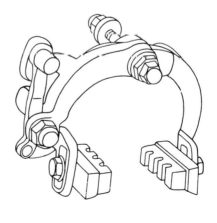

The Universal Super 68 Side-pull brake set is a quality brake suitable for a variety of uses and is much, much cheaper than Campagnolo's.

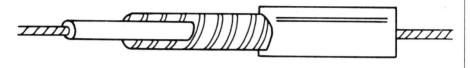

Teflon-coated cables may sound like a strange idea, but it's a good one. They never need lubrication because the Teflon coating eliminates the friction between the metal cable and the plastic housing.

BRAKE AND DERAILLEUR CABLES

Best by Far: You probably never thought about your cables and their housings. But you can improve the feel and convenience of your bike by using Teflon-coated cables that come matched with vinyl- or plastic-lined housings. Such an arrangement can cut friction by 40 percent, and eliminates the bother of trying to lubricate your cables by sneaking drops of oil inside the housings (an almost impossible task). We won't recommend specific brands, because they tend to appear and disappear with suddenness. Just ask for Teflon cables. They're a replacement-part item, definitely not found as standard equipment on any bicycle we've heard of.

A Good Buy: Your best, and obvious, buy is to stick with the standard cables that come with your derailleurs and brakes. They come as part of the package price, so they don't cost anything extra.

BRAKE SHOES

Best by Far: There's a clear winner in this category: Mathauser brake shoes. These shoes are larger than standard shoes and are curved to fit the wheel rim. They're also totally flat on their pressing surfaces, which theoretically gives them more stopping power in the rain. The flat pads have a squeegee effect, wiping the rim dry when they're applied. The solid part of Mathauser shoes are made of finned aluminum. These fins help dissipate heat build-up. Standard shoes can heat up dangerously on steep descents, causing their pads to leave a thin glaze on the rim, making stopping less effective. Manufacturers of Mathauser shoes claim their product isn't bothered by this problem. We've been very satisfied with these brake shoes and found them worth their very high price; the only discouraging words have come from some racers who think they stop the bike too quickly. But this shouldn't be a problem for most of us, especially tourists who have lots of weight on the bike and need the stopping power.

A Good Buy: We recommend that you just use the shoes that come standard with your bike. But eventually, these will wear out, and a good, cheap replacement brand is Weinmann. Weinmann shoes are readily available, and they work well.

PEDALS

Think about how many times you rotate your feet during a day's ride and you'll realize how much wear and tear your pedals have to endure. With an occasional lubrication and tightening, a good set of pedals—barring any accident—should last the lifetime of your bike.

Best by Far: Once again it's the Italians, the Campagnolo company, that hold the lead in this component. If you decide to take the plunge and get the ultimate set of pedals and if you don't mind spending a lot of money, the ultimate bicycling pedal is the Campagnolo Super Record Road Black pedal with a black anodized finish for looks and a titanium spindle for lightness.

A Good Buy: For about one tenth the price of the Campagnolo pedals, you can get a set of Lyotard 136 pedals, which are plain chromed-steel. While they may not last the lifetime of your bike, they can be replaced seven or eight times and you still wouldn't have paid for them what you would on the Campagnolo's. They do what they're supposed to do, they require little routine maintenance, and they are inexpensive.

CRANKS AND CHAINWHEELS

While cranks and chainwheels may be bought separately, getting a matched set is recommended because not all brands of chainwheels are compatible with all brands of cranks. It's also convenient to get the same brand of bottom bracket. The whole assembly —cranks, chainwheels, and bottom bracket—is commonly called the *crankset.*

Best by Far: And the best made is Campagnolo. Like other Campagnolo products, their cranksets are light, strong, finely made, and beautiful. They are expensive—but they are not the most expensive available. Other European brands—such as Stronglight and Avocet—have surpassed them in price and lightness. But not, we think, in quality and dependability. The Campagnolo Nuovo Record cranks may be purchased with Nuovo Record chainrings or with the lighter —and more expensive—Super Record chainrings. Both are good; it's just a matter of whether or not you want to spend the extra money for the Super Record's approximately 20 grams of weight savings.

A Good Buy: The T.A. Cyclotouriste crankset makes good sense for most cycle tourists. Besides being about one third cheaper than Campi, T.A. cranksets has a huge range of chainwheels to choose from. They're available in sizes from 26 to 55 teeth (compared to 42 to 55 teeth for Campagnolo and most other competition chainwheels). Also, T.A. replacement parts are widely available.

CHAINS

You can cancel out the benefits of having all the best components on a bike if you skimp on the kind of chain you get. Even the best of chains are relatively inexpensive items so don't try to save a little money by buying less than the best.

The Uniglide 11 chain eliminates the need to overshift when gear shifting. Its widened outerplates keep the chain from slipping over the teeth of the desired gear.

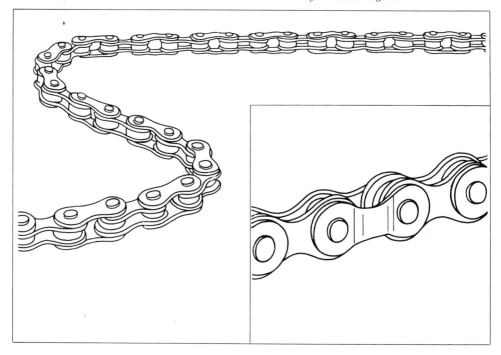

Best by Far: What is the best? That's open to some discussion, but we and many others feel that Regina is the best brand of chains. If you're a millionaire, you can invest in their all-time chain, but we feel it is an exorbitant and rather unnecessary purchase. We think the best Regina chain out now for the money is the Regina Oro, which is made of steel- and brass-plated links. The brass finish resists corrosion and interacts with a minimum of friction with the steel parts of the links giving your pedaling a smooth, liquid feel. You really have to try it to get the full sensation of this unique design.

A Good Buy: A less-expensive alternate to the Regina Oro chain is the Uniglide Chain sold by the Japanese company, Shimano. It's extremely durable—it doesn't stretch out as soon as other brands—and it has a unique feature in the links that fit over the teeth on your front sprocket and rear gear cluster. Each link is slightly bowed or widened, with the result that people who use it say that it shifts much more smoothly and is less prone to "skip" over gears when going from a lower to higher gear or back down. As a second choice, it is an excellent one.

FRONT DERAILLEURS

Best by Far: Campagnolo, again, makes the best model here. Racers swear by the Campagnolo derailleur, and tourists like it because it's not only smooth but dependable. There are much lighter derailleurs made, but none better. Even when clogged with mud and grit, it still shifts reliably. It is still the most expensive, however.

A Good Buy: The Sun Tour Cyclone is much cheaper than the Campagnolo, is actually lighter, and works fairly smoothly. We like it a little better than the other popular Japanese derailleur, the Shimano. The Cyclone does not hold up well under poor conditions, however. Sun Tour also makes a Cyclone GT, which is a touring model equipped to handle large variations in gears.

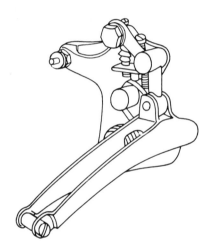

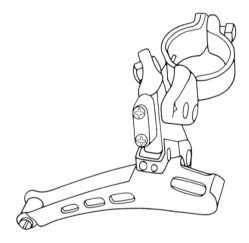

Campagnolo, as always, makes both the best and the most expensive piece of equipment. Their front derailleur, with its parallelogram design, steel cage, and hinged body, is both reliable and smooth.

The Shimano-500 EC-500 front derailleur is steel with a satin nickel finish. Nearly twice as heavy as the Campagnolo or the Sun Tour Cyclone, it is still fairly dependable and workable.

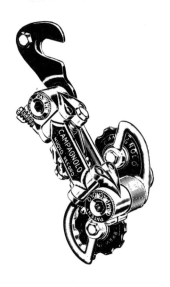

The Campagnolo Nuovo Record rear derailleur (above) won't flex during shifting and is very precise, extremely strong, and highly reliable. The Sun Tour Cyclone derailleur (below) offers the "slant pantograph" design and a "straight pull" feature for the cable, which results in less wear on the cable and a positive feel when shifting.

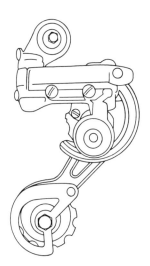

REAR DERAILLEURS

Best by Far: Campagnolo again has set the standard in derailleurs for decades. While some of the Japanese rear derailleurs may be better designed, none work with its fluidity or sureness. Its only limitation is that it's rated to be used with rear cogs no larger than 28 teeth, though we once coupled it with a 30-tooth gear with no problem. Campagnolo derailleurs are made for racers. Tourists, who commonly need gears of 34 or even more teeth, must settle for other models. The Campi we're talking about is the Nuovo Record. As expensive as it is, there's an even more expensive model called the Super Record. While it looks quite different, the Super Record is basically the same as the Nuovo Record except that it uses titanium pivot bolts, which lowers its weight by about 20 grams (and raises its price considerably). Unless you race, you're probably better off with the Nuovo Record.

A Good Buy: The Sun Tour Cyclone is half the price of a Campagnolo, and perhaps only half as good. Still, it's better than anything else. One possible drawback is the Cyclone lever set. It's extremely light, and that can be a problem. The levers sometimes have trouble holding the derailleur in the proper gear unless tightened very hard. The assembly that holds the levers to the down tube is also rather flimsy. You might be better off with the standard Sun Tour lever set, which is much less expensive but more solid. The Cyclone derailleur also comes in a GT model, a touring design that will handle cogs up to 34 teeth. (The regular Cyclone is rated only to 24 teeth.)

REAR FREEWHEEL CLUSTERS

Best by Far: The Regina Super Corsa Oro freewheel with five or six cogs (this whole assembly is commonly called a cluster) is the model preferred by most racers, and it's good for the rest of us as well. The Regina is smooth, light, and long wearing. The Super Corsa Oro also has an interesting feature: its hardened steel cogs are brass-plated. This is not just for looks —brass and steel tend to resist each other because of their molecular makeup, and this means that the steel chain will shift more smoothly over a brass-plated cluster. The Regina is actually less expensive than some of its high-priced Japanese competition.

A Good Buy: Sun Tour's Pro Compe cluster is not only a good buy for those who want to save some money, but also for tourists who need lower gears. The Regina cluster cannot be had with cogs with over 28 teeth. The Pro Compe offers cogs with up to 34 teeth.

SEAT POSTS

The seat post is one of the most underrated and forgotten components of the bicycle. So much of how comfortable you are and how efficiently you pedal, for example, depends on the correct seat height and position. If your seat post can't hold your saddle in your favorite position, you can get pretty bored by continually adjusting and readjusting it.

Best by Far: The Campagnolo Super Record post is a beautifully tooled component precision-made to fit solidly and snugly in your frame's seat tube, yet adjusts easily and effortlessly. You don't need a lot of muscle to make adjustments in this, and when you do, it holds.

A Good Buy: Not quite as elegant looking as the Campagnolo design but still smooth functioning, is the Sakae Ringyo seat post. It is easy to adjust, strong, and just about as dependable a component as the Campagnolo. There are just two differences: It doesn't carry the Campagnolo name or the price tag.

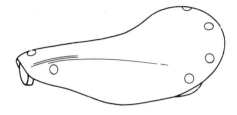

The Ideale #90 Special Competition saddle (directly below) is professional quality with a two-wire frame and top quality leather.

Avocet's touring saddle for women is a unique and sensible accommodation to the differences between men's and women's pelvic structures.

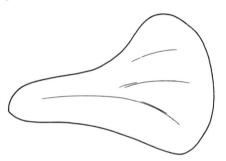

SADDLES

If you plan to spend a lot on any one accessory on your bike, next to a good set of derailleurs, it should be your saddle. A decent saddle can make all the difference not only in how efficiently you pedal but how comfortable you feel as well. Cheap saddles never get comfortable, but get saggy and deformed with heavy use and will in the end leave you with painful memories. Unlike most other bike components, a good saddle will mold itself to your individual shape and can be easily transferred from one bike to the next. Some saddles even appreciate in value and become sought after precisely because they are used and broken in. Any good saddle should last the lifetime of the average nonprofessional rider who will be sitting on it.

Best by Far: Considered by us to be the best at any price is the French-made Ideale 90 Competition saddle. It's made of firm but pliable thick leather and is preoiled to give you almost instant comfort from the moment you sit on it. There is no painful breaking-in period with these saddles. They are so well made, with brass rivets and steel frames, that they are virtually indestructable.

A Good Buy: As comfortable, but we feel not quite as durable, is our budget choice for the bicyclist: the Avocet touring saddles. These are unique in that the company makes a male and female version. The men's saddle is the typically narrow teardrop shape while the woman's is slightly wider to accommodate the wider pelvic structure of the woman cyclist. For a wide-framed woman who has not found any other saddle comfortable, this might be the answer to her prayers. Women with narrower hips might want to try both versions before deciding which one to buy.

PUMPS

You can spend a small fortune on bicycle pumps and still end up with a piece of junk. For some reason, the range of quality in this accessory goes from excellent to totally useless. The higher pressure your tires take, the stronger and better-made pump you will have to use. In this category we have really two kinds of bests.

Best by Far—two types: The first is the kind of pump you would keep at home to pump up your tires for a day's ride. This is a T-handle pump with a long hose, called the floor pump. For the high-pressure sew-up tires with Presta valves, the best type available is the Silca floor. It comes with its own built-in air pressure gauge and, if you're daring enough, will let you pump as much as 170 pounds (16 kilograms) of air pressure into your tires with hardly any effort.

As far as the ideal bicycle pump to carry around with you is concerned, the best by far is the Zefal High Pressure pump. It has a unique thumb-lock lever that clamps the end of the pump over the bicycle valve and eliminates using a hose at all, so you don't have to struggle unscrewing the hose from a tire before all the air leaks out. It makes pumping, even high-pressure tires, unbelievably simple and, best of all, is adaptable for use with either Presta or Schraeder valves.

The Silca floor pump (left) is the best high-pressure pump available, extremely efficient and capable of pumping to 170 lbs. To inflate sew-ups, unscrew the valve stem counter clockwise a few turns, then test to make sure the valve is open by punching the stem inwards to see if it lets out air. It can be used with presta valves only. The Zefal high-pressure pump (right) has a thumb lock that prevents air loss when applying or removing the pump. It is much less exerting to use than the Silca and can be adapted to use with either presta or schrader valves.

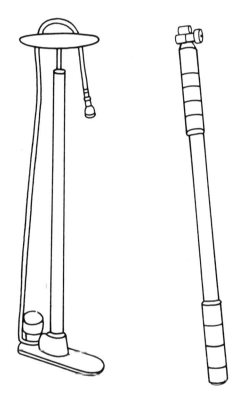

HELMETS

Only the Best: Everyone agrees bicyclists should wear helmets, but no one agrees on the type. Only in the past few years has anyone bothered to concentrate on improving on the traditional hairnet style helmet worn by most professional racers. As a result, there's been an explosion of designs in headgear protection for the cyclist. Some of it is fine, some of it is mediocre, and some of it is a waste of money.

The best kinds of helmet are the hard plastic types, but one of the problems with most of them is that while they give decent head protection, they can also be suffocatingly hot on warm or even cool days. One helmet that we think avoids this problem is a unique design called the Skid Lid II. It's an openwork-style helmet made of hard plastic with a shock-resistant foam liner and a chin strap to hold it in place. It gives full protection to the sides and upper part of the skull but has large gaps between the wide plastic slats that curve up over part of the top of the head. The design is based on the discovery that most head injuries in bicycling happen to the sides of the skull and rarely, if ever, to the top. It gives protection plus enough ventilation to keep you cool.

Since we don't believe you should scrimp on helmets, we won't recommend a budget model, but we will offer a second choice. Not quite as comfortable, but very protective, is the Bell Bicycle Helmet made expressly for bicycling by a company with years of prior experience in making motorcycle helmets. It costs almost as much as the Skid Lid II, but since it is not quite as cool to wear, we placed it as our second choice.

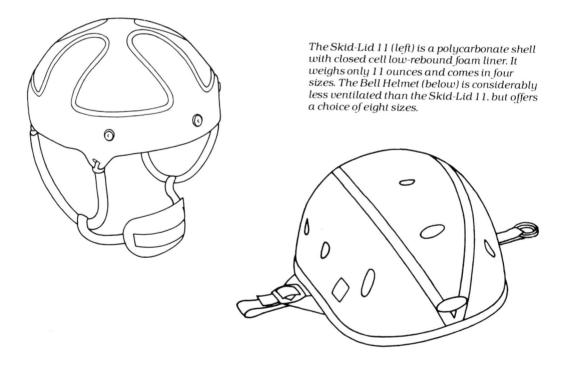

The Skid-Lid 11 (left) is a polycarbonate shell with closed cell low-rebound foam liner. It weighs only 11 ounces and comes in four sizes. The Bell Helmet (below) is considerably less ventilated than the Skid-Lid 11, but offers a choice of eight sizes.

BIKE LOCKS

Best by Far: The best bike lock is a solid piece of through-hardened metal with a hard-to-pick lock built right inside. The best example we know of this is the Citadel bicycle lock, a U-shaped bar of tough metal with a locking bar that slips onto the open end of the U. This forms one of the toughest bicycle locks now available. The lock is a smooth round bar, which makes it hard for a thief with bolt cutters to get a good bite and cut through. It is also through-hardened, meaning that practically nothing short of an acetylene torch could cut through metal this hard very quickly or easily. If you have an expensive bike you want to park and protect, this is one of the best locks you can buy.

A Good Buy: Even the Citadel lock isn't perfect, however. It is heavy and will only clamp to narrow posts such as those used for street signs. If you are looking for a light-weight alternative, a not-bad budget choice is a lock with a case-hardened shackle and a coil of what is sometimes called air-craft cable—a thick, plastic-coated steel rope with a loop at either end. This combination is lighter than the Citadel and offers you the option of locking your bike to a large pole or some odd-sized fixed object. This combination is also good for the traveling bicyclists who want some security for their bikes but don't want to carry around all that heavy metal. It won't give you the same bike protection as the Citadel, so you should make an effort to use it to chain your bike up in a public place where you can keep your eye on it.

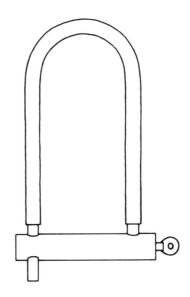

The Citadel lock is made of ½-inch Thru-hardened alloy, is vinyl-coated, and comes with a one-year, $200-theft guarantee. Aircraft cable with a case-hardened shackle offers a lighter and cheaper alternative (below).

CARRYING RACKS

For heavy-duty touring where you will be carrying a lot of weight around on the back of your bike in the form of loaded panniers and maybe a tent and sleeping bag, you should get the strongest, sturdiest carrying rack available.

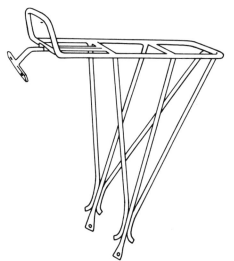
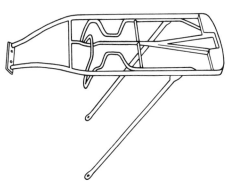

The Blackburn carrier rack (left) is the best there is for heavy-duty use. The Pletscher rack (right) is more suitable for lightweight touring.

Best by Far: And that is the Blackburn luggage carrier. It's light, made totally of aluminum, but because of its special reinforced structure, extremely strong as well. It's welded together and offers a stiff, solid support for whatever you might want to load on it. Unlike other racks, it doesn't sway when loaded and won't make for shaky riding when you go cycling.

A Good Buy: Not bad for lightweight touring or just carrying odds and ends, is the cheaper Pletscher rack. It, too, is made of aluminum and also comes with a spring clamp to hold your load in place. Although it will tend to sway when really loaded down, it is a perfect all-around bike rack and at about a third of the price of a Blackburn rack, a good bargain.

HANDLEBAR BAGS

The best rule of thumb in shopping for handlebar bags is to buy the smallest model you think you will need. Having a big bag only tempts you to fill up all that room with all kinds of extra stuff that you ordinarily would leave behind and probably will never use on your trip.

The T.A. Handlebar Bag, made in France, is made of tough water-repellant canvas and is designed to be accessible while you're riding.

Best by Far: If you do have some self-restraint and are looking for a top handlebar bag, one with plenty of room that you can carry off the bike as a shoulderbag, our choice for the best is the Cannondale Trestle Front Bag. It has five pockets on the outside, three dividers on the inside, and a clear-plastic map case where you can keep your map handy and still protect it from the weather.

A Good Buy: Less exotic and a little smaller, is the TA Handlebar Bag, which has two outside compartments and plenty of room for tools, a spare tire or tube, and maybe a light lunch on a day trip. It's not fancy or modern-looking—it's made of canvas instead of plastic—but it is well-designed.

PANNIERS

Best by Far: As with handlebar bags, there are many well-made panniers on the market, but our favorite remains the Tourist Cyclist panniers for the best choice. They are sturdily made of heavy-duty, waterproof nylon; are equipped with handy outside pockets big enough to carry gear for a 6-month or year trip if you are that ambitious; and they have other added features such as the special shoulder strap included with them and the handy feature that allows the pair of bags to zip together, back to back. Other bags have been modeled along the same lines, but none have duplicated the quality.

A Good Buy: If you're looking for a set of relatively inexpensive, small panniers, say for a weekend trip, check out the Bellwether 1202 Rear Touring Panniers. The Bellwether company has had years of experience designing bicycle bags and these are a reasonably priced, well-made sample of that experience. These, too, have handy outside pockets and can be adjusted to fit any type of rear carrier your bike might have. For the price of these bags, it's hard to find anything as good.

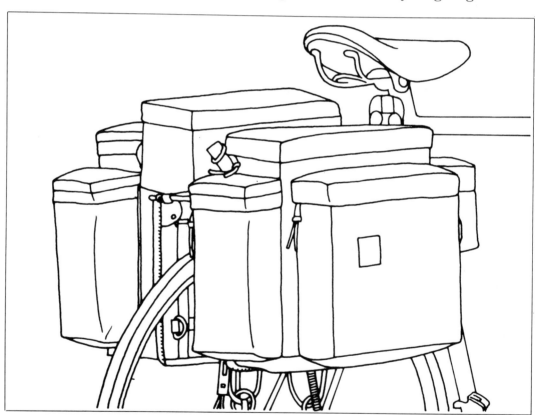

The Bellwether 1202 Rear Touring Panniers have easy-to-use velcro fasteners and are adjustable to fit all rear carriers. The underside is made of abrasion-resistant cordora nylon, and the outside is waterproofed nylon oxford.

LIGHTS

No bicycle light made will do a tremendously efficient job of lighting your way as you pedal at night. For that reason, we recommend you avoid night riding at all costs. If you want the psychological security of having some light, the first thing you should do is buy an armband light such as the one illustrated on page 57 in Chapter 4.

Best by Far: Your first priority when riding at night should be to be seen. That done, you might want to invest in a light you could use as a kind of bike headlight on the bike and a handy flashlight off the bike. Probably the brightest and most compact of the battery-operated models now out is one called the Berec Headlight. It gives the broadest beam of any battery light and is easily detachable from the bike-frame mounting bracket that comes with it.

A Good Buy: A good second-choice light is an ingenious model called the Wonder Light. It comes with a cleverly designed holder-clamp that attaches to the frame of handlebars and is packaged in a tough waterproof case. Its one drawback is that it uses special batteries which can sometimes be difficult to find.

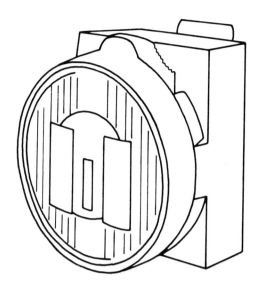

The Berc headlight (top) is made of durable A.B.S. plastic with a wide lens that has excellent dispersion. The Wonder headlight (bottom) has a universal mounting bracket that fits all bikes and can be adjusted to any position. It's impact proof and waterproof.

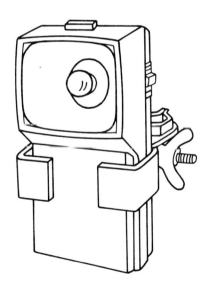

APPENDIX

Useful Addresses and Suppliers:

Calculating Your Gear Ratios

I. NORTH AMERICA— ORGANIZATIONS

UNITED STATES

American Youth Hostels, Inc.
National Campus
Delaplane, VA 22025
Contrary to what you might assume from its title, AYH has no upper age limit for members. With chapters all over the U.S., AYH sponsors local, national, and international bicycle tours and is a handy source of information for the solo bicycling tourist.

Bikecentennial
P. O. Box 8308
Missoula, MT 59807
A national, non-profit bicycling organization that sponsors tours across all or parts of the U.S. and is also a valuable source of maps and other bike touring information. Its resource pamphlet, *The Cyclists' Yellow Pages*, alone is worth the price of membership ($15).

League of American Wheelmen (LAW)
10 East Read Street
Baltimore, MD 21202
This bike organization has the bicycling commuter's interest at heart. One of the earliest bike organizations in the U.S., LAW works hard at lobbying for bike lanes at local levels and upgrading existing lanes. If that's your interest, this is the organization.

United States Cycling Federation
1750 East Boulder
Colorado Springs, Co. 80909
The organization for amateur bicycle racing in the United States. If you plan to get serious about racing, then write to the USCF for their membership information.

CANADA

Canadian Cycling Association
333 River Road
Vanier, Ottawa, K1l 8B9

ORGANIZATIONS FOR EUROPEAN TOURS

American Youth Hostels, Inc.
(see address above)

Bike Dreams Tours, Inc.
P.O. Box 20653
Houston, TX 77025

International Bicycle Touring Society
2115 Paseo Dorado
LaJolla, CA 92037

Out Spokin' Bicycling Organization
Box 370
Elkhart, IN 46515

Spinning Spokes, Inc.
8405 SW 160th Street
Miami, FL 33157

MAP SOURCES

American Youth Hostels, Inc.
(see address above)
Has tours mapped out for both Europe and the U.S.

Bikecentennial
(see address above)
Has a cross-country route mapped out expressly for cyclists in the United States as well as detailed regional bike routes for many different areas of the country.

U.S. Geological Survey
This government organization sells highly detailed contour maps of tremendous value to the traveling cyclist. Specify the 1:250,000 series when you write for a free map index.

For maps of states east of the Mississippi River, write to:
U.S. Geological Survey
1200 South Eads Street
Arlington, VA 22202

For maps of states west of the Mississippi River, write to:
U.S. Geological Survey
Box 25286 Federal Center
Denver, CO 80225

Rand McNally
P.O. Box 7600
Chicago, IL 60680
This map company not only has an extensive selection of maps for both the U.S. and Europe, it also has a decent selection of guidebooks on campgrounds in Europe and the U.S. Although these are not expressly designed for the bicyclist, they do offer valuable traveling advice.

Bartholomew maps of the British Isles are available from Rand McNally

Michelin maps, guide books and booklets can be found in large book stores or ordered by mail from:

French and European
    Publications, Inc.
115 Fifth Ave.
New York, NY 10020

EQUIPMENT SOURCES

The following are some addresses of the better equipment sources in the United States.

Eastern Mountain Sports
14201 Vose Farm Rd.
Peterborough, NH 03450

Green Mountain Schwinn Cyclery
133 Strong Ave
Rutland, VT 05701

Carl Hart Bicycles
9 Middle Country Road
Rt 25, Middle Island, NY 11953

Bikes and Things
377 East 23 St
New York, NY 10010

Stuyvesant Bicycle
349 West 14 St
New York, NY 10014

Toga Bike Shop
229 Avenue B
New York, NY 10009

Metropolitan New York Council
American Youth Hostels
132 Spring St.
New York, NY 10012

Pete's Bike Shop
Highway 31
Flemington, NJ 08822

Pedal Pushers Inc.
1130 Rogero Road
Jacksonville, FL 32211

International Pro Bike Shop
3733 Wilmington Pike
OH 45429

Bike Warehouse
215 Main Street
New Middleton, OH 44442

Cyclo-Pedia
122 S. Main
Mount Pleasant, MI 48858

Eclipse, Inc.
P.O. Box 372
Ann Arbor, MI 48107

Cycle Goods Corp
2735 Hennepin Ave South
Minneapolis, MN 55408

Kirtland/Tourpak
Box 4059 Boulder, CO 80302

The Touring Cyclist Shop
P.O. Box 4009
Boulder, CO 80306

Gerry Division
Outdoor Sports Industries, Inc.
5450 N. Valley Highway
Denver, CO 80216

Hartley Alley's Touring Cyclist Shop
2639 Spruce Street
Boulder, CO 80306

Sierra Specialties
1850 Bonneville Ave
Reno, Nevada 89503

Tempe Bicycle Shop
602 South Mill
Tempe, AZ 85281

The Bicycle Outfitter
2089 Sunset
Pacific Grove, CA 93950

Two Wheel Transit Authority
318 Main
Huntington Beach, CA 92648

Palo Alto Bicycles
171 University Ave.
Palo Alto, CA 94302

Bikecology
2910 Nebraska Ave.
P.O. Box 1880
Santa Monica, CA 90406

Bellwether
1161 Mission St.
San Francisco, CA 94103

CANADA
Ramsay's Bicycles
201 Lakeshore Rd East
Mississauga
Ontario, Canada L5G 2G1

Peel Bicycle Centre
1832 Ste Catherine West
Montreal
Quebec H3H 1M1

Bicyclesport
175 King Street East
Toronto
Ontario M5A 1J4

II. EUROPE— ORGANIZATIONS

The kinds of services these organizations offer the cyclist will vary from one country to another. At the very least, they have newsletters where various tours are publicized or where riders looking for traveling companions will advertise. Many are excellent sources of maps for their countries and some, such as the Cyclists' Touring Club in England, even have maps of tours customized for the cyclist. When you write, they will notify you of the range of their services.

AUSTRIA
Osterreichischer Automobil, Motorad und Touring Club
Schubertring 3
1011 Vienna

BELGIUM
Royal Belgian Touring Club
44 rue de la Loi
1041 Bruxelles

DENMARK
Dansk Cyklist Forbund
Kjeld Langes Gade 14
DK—1367

ENGLAND, SCOTLAND, and WALES
British Cycling Federation
70 Brompton Road
London SW3 1EN
In addition to being the main amateur racing organization in the United Kingdom, the BCF also provides its members with third-party insurance and touring information.

Cyclists' Touring Club
Cottrell House
69 Meadow
Godalming, Surrey
GU7 3HS

Founded in 1888, the CTC is the premier touring organization and over the years has amassed an elaborate listing of detailed bicycle maps of specific tours of Ireland, the British Isles, and the Continent.

GERMANY
Allgemeiner Deutscher Automobil-Club
Baumgartnerstrasse 53
Munich 70

GREECE
Automobile Touring Club of Greece
2-4 Messogion Street
Athens 610

ITALY
Touring Club Italiano
Corso Italia 10
20122 Milan

THE NETHERLANDS
Koninklijke Nederlandsche Toeristenbond
Wassenaarseweg 220
Den Haag
They offer cycle tour maps and package cycle tours of Holland.

Stichting:Fiets!
Europaplein 2
1078 GZ Amsterdam
A smaller cycling organization, Stichting:Fiets! also provides cycling maps of Holland and in addition has information booklets on firms that rent bicycles and information on cycling in that country.

NORWAY
Syklistenes Landsforening
Wesselsgatan 8   Oslo 1

SPAIN
Real Automobil Club de Espana
General Sanjurjo 10
Madrid 3

SWEDEN
Cykelframjandet
Stora Nygatan
Stockholm 111 21

SWITZERLAND
Touring Club Suisse
rue Pierre-Fatio 9
1211 Geneva

MAP SOURCES

There are really only two addresses you need to know for getting maps of the United Kingdom and the Continent. They are:

John Bartholomew & Son
12 Duncan St.
Edinburgh, Scotland
EH1 1TA

and for Michelin road maps of the Continent write to:

Pneu Michelin
46 Ave. de Breteuil
Paris

With these sources and the cycling organization for a specific country, you will have access to all the maps you will need.

BICYCLING EQUIPMENT

For panniers:

Carradice of Nelson, Ltd.
Brook St.
Nelson
Lancashire, BB9 9PX
U.K.

Karrimor Weathertite Products, Ltd.
Avenue Parade
Accrington
Lancashire, U.K.

Frame builders:

Mercian Cycles Ltd
28 Stenson Rd
Cavendish, Derby DE3 7JB

Bob Jackson
148 Harehills Lane
Leeds, LS8 5BD

Woodrup Cycles
345 Kirkstall Road
Leeds

Condor Cycles
144-148 Gray's Inn Road
London WC1 8AA

F.W. Evans
77-79 The Cut
Waterloo, London SE1

Jack Taylor Cycles
Church Street
Stockton, Tyne and Wear
Cleveland County TS18 2LY

Mail order sources for bicycles and accessories:

ENGLAND
Biped
Dept. CTI
P.O. Box 8
Nelson
BB9 9RW
U.K.

Freewheel
275 West End Lane
London NW6 1QS
U.K.

Ron Kitching
Hookstone Park Harrogate
Yorkshire
U.K.

FRANCE
JPR
17 rue du Phalanstere
38000 Grenoble
France

Stand 21
10 rue Charles-Brifaut
21000 Dijon
France

ITALY
Cinelli Cino
Via Egidio Folli 45
Milano 20134

Guerciotti
Via Petrella 4
Milano 20124

CALCULATING YOUR GEAR RATIOS

Knowing the relative sizes of your gears not only enables you to compare the performance of different gearing arrangements, but also allows you to make sure that your existing system uses all the gears most efficiently. By calculating the power of each of the permutations on a ten-speed bike, for example, you can check that none of the gears duplicate each other. Your top gear on your small front chainwheel, for example, may be exactly equivalent to combining your large front chainwheel with a fairly low rear sprocket.

The size of a gear is calculated by multiplying the number of teeth on your front chainwheel by the size of your wheels (usually 27 inches) and dividing the result by the number of teeth on the rear sprocket. This result is expressed in inches. For example, a 48-tooth front chainwheel and a 16-tooth rear sprocket on a 27-inch wheeled bicycle, produces the following calculation:

$$\frac{48 \times 27}{16} = 81$$

that is, a gear ratio of 81. The table opposite gives gear ratios (rounded to the nearest inch) for most combinations on a 27-inch wheeled bike.

In Europe, gear ratios are calculated using the circumference of the wheel, not the diameter, so these measurements cannot be converted directly into a metric gear ratio.

For most purposes, a front chainwheel of 52 is large enough. With a rear top cog of 13, this gives a top gear of 108—easily high enough for most racing events. Generally, racing bikes have something like a 52-44 front combination and a rear freewheel cluster with a top of 13 (or sometimes even 12) with one, or even two tooth jumps to the lowest sprocket, depending on the type of event or the nature of the course. A typical touring bike would have a front chainwheel combination of 52-36, and rear freewheel cluster ranging from 14 to 26 teeth.

GEAR RATIO CHART

TEETH ON REAR COG

TEETH ON CHAINRING

	24	23	22	21	20	19	18	17	16	15	14	13
40	45	47	49	51	54	57	60	64	68	72	77	83
42	47	49	52	54	57	60	63	67	71	76	81	87
44	50	52	54	57	59	63	66	70	74	79	85	91
45	51	53	55	58	61	64	68	71	76	81	87	93
46	52	54	56	59	62	65	69	73	78	83	89	96
47	53	55	58	60	63	67	71	75	79	85	91	98
48	54	56	59	62	65	68	72	76	81	86	93	100
49	55	58	60	63	66	70	74	78	83	88	95	102
50	56	59	61	64	68	71	75	79	84	90	96	104
51	57	60	63	66	69	72	77	81	86	92	98	106
52	59	61	64	67	70	74	78	83	88	94	100	108
53	60	62	65	68	72	75	80	84	89	95	102	110
54	61	63	66	69	73	77	81	86	91	97	104	112
55	62	65	68	71	74	78	83	87	93	99	106	114
56	63	66	69	72	76	80	84	89	95	101	108	116

INDEX

Quarto would also like to thank:
Elizabeth Fox; Gene Santoro; Ella Stewart; Jim Walker; Donna Sturm;
and TI Raleigh and Stuyvesant Bicycle for their generous help.

Picture credits:

Elizabeth Fox: 8, 102, 126
Bikecentennial/Rich Lander: 68
Bikecentennial: 54
Greg Siple: 44
TI Raleigh (USA): 28, 86